The letters of Thomas Lovell Beddoes

ISBN: 0692397671

Curious Books
Florida, USA

The Letters of
Thomas Lovell Beddoes

Edited with notes

by Edmond Gosse

Curious Books, USA

Prefatory Note

By publishing the correspondence contained in this volume, I conclude the performance of a duty laid upon me by the late Mr. Robert Browning.

It is not necessary that I should here repeat in detail the circumstances of the transference of these papers to Mr. Browning by the will of Mr. Thomas Forbes Kelsall in 1872. All information on this point will be found given minutely in the preface to my edition of the Poetical Worlds of Beddoes (J. M. Dent & Co., 1890. 2 vols.). It suffices to say that it was the wish of Kelsall, at whose absolute disposal all the MSS. of Beddoes were placed by the poet's death-bed memorandum, that these letters should be published, at a proper interval after the death of Miss Zoë King, an event which took place twelve years ago. Large use was made of the correspondence by Kelsall himself when he compiled the memoir of Beddoes which was prefixed to the Poems of 1851, but this is the first time that the letters are textually published, while the volume of 1851 has never been reprinted, and has now become rare. A few of these letters, those addressed to B. W. Procter, were published by my friend Mr. Coventry Patmore in his anonymous memoir of that writer. Another was given to myself by the late Mrs. Procter. I have to thank Mr. Robert Barrett Browning for the kindness with which he confirmed his father's wish that I should publish these papers, the originals of the remainder of which are now in his possession.

Few collections of letters exist in which the discussion of literary topics holds so prominent a place as it does in these of Beddoes. If any excuse were needed for bringing them before the public, it would be more than supplied by Mr. Swinburne, who, as long ago as 1875, remarked of the *author of* Death's Jest Book *that his "noble instinct for poetry" was better shown in his letters than even in his practice as a verse-writer, and added that Beddoes' "brilliant correspondence on poetical questions gives to me a higher view of his fine and vigorous intelligence than any other section of his literary remains."*

It is the letters which were thus distinguished which are here presented to the public.

E. G.

December, 1893.

To Thomas Forbes Kelsall

2 Devereux C^t.
A Sunday in Feb^y [1824]

Dear Kelsall,—Being on the edge of a journey deep into the country for a fortnight, and altogether desperate of receiving any official answer from Mr. J. Hunt,(1) I write to inform you how the Shelley(2) affair goes on. On Mr. Waller's receiving your answer he brought it here and we in full assembly with your paper proxy declared for 250 copies. I was installed secretary and wrote on the spot to J. Hunt informing him that we offered to become responsible for so many, and adding that it was out of our power to do any more. This was nearly, if not quite, a month ago. I have received no answer; but Mr. Hunt has written to Procter(3) about it, saying that he had already mentioned 500 copies to Mrs. Shelley; that 250 copies will *not* pay for printing & advertisements; and that we ought to give her a chance of getting something, or perhaps she would not like to publish &c &c.

Very true, very likely, very plausible, Mr. John Hunt. For the twinkling of this very distant chance we three poor honest admirers of Shelley's poetry are certainly to pay: if all, a few, as many more who have professed the same would do as much in proportion to their power, nothing would be better than to print 500 or 750 copies (if it pleases the Gods of wastepaper,) for Mr. J. Hunt to sell at twopence a pound three or four years hence. Besides if they want to double our number what hinders them. Here is our offer to pay all the foundation expenses of the printing, and the whole of the advertising; now if so much is to be made of the latter 250, if they are so marvellously alchemical, can no other person venture the comparative trifle they are to cost. But "if it is a trifle then," says my opponent, "why cannot you, the 'honest

1

admirer' spare this trifle?" Because I know it will be thrown away; I have gone quite far enough, I never intended to go further any more than to retreat; all that I can afford is offered. Take it, Mr. J. Hunt or reject it, as you please; if it were in a matter of less import, if it were for any other sublunary purpose I wd have withdrawn it long ago, feeling that we have not been treated in the way, which our disinterestedness deserved; to a certain extent in this case I will submit to be "made a convenience of."

What they intend to do is beyond my knowledge or conjecture; very probably the publisher or printer is only trying to double his job, & when the attempt fails will proceed contentedly as he may. Are not Simpkin & Marshall now selling the remainder of Ollier's 250 copies of his best(4) poems at a reduction of 70 per cent? "I'll go no further."

Have you seen the "Westminster"? Procter has cut it; they did certainly not behave very well to him; and he holds to the "Edinburgh"—a falling house. This new review deserves support, the internal support of talent I mean, & then the other will follow of course, for it's principle. It dissects the "Edinburgh." well enough, and alludes to a celebrated cousin of yours in one article as "a stripling who can write a readable article for a magazine" &c Who wrote not Paul but Jesus? Not Smith but Austen; Mr. Knight's Austen is Mr Hunt's Gamaliel.

There was a new intolerable opera the other night at Covent-garden, with Miss Tree in a nice new pair of white silk pantaloons. Chas. Kemble is to come out in Falstaff and they have under cover a new tragedy (Shiel or Walkers(5) or some of those immortals we conjecture;) and, credite posteri, a new comedy with songs.

Spenser—you do him injustice; I was and am villainously ignorant of him; but I have bought him in folio and intend to read him piece-meal. Beginning, as all rational folks do, at the end, I stumbled on "Britain's Ida";(6) which is extremely like Keats with a mixture of the Shakspearian play on words. I picked up Daniel too, who is certainly an unconquerable Alp of weariness, his tragedies would have delighted Voltaire: they are a good deal worse than "Cato." I have finished the first act of a play; oh! so stupid. Procter has the brass to tell me he likes that fool the last man.(7) I shall go on with neither; there are now three first acts in my drawer when I have got two more I shall stitch them together, and stick the sign of a fellow tweedling a mask in his fingers, with "good entertainment for man and ass" understood as the grammarians (not the Chrestomathic ones,) say. You'll think this letter comes from old Bernard the Quaker(8) it's so like a wounded snake, but it proceeds from the proper paw of

Yours truly

T. L. Beddoes.

The Ring. Thank you; the old woman's taken in tho',—it is not a diamond—but dear me how I keep you from your clients!

Addressed to
        Thomas Kelsall Esqre
           Hound well Lane
              Southampton

To Bryan Waller Procter
Bristol, March 3rd, 1824

Dear Procter,—I have just been reading your epistle to our Ajax Flagellifer, the bloody John Lacy:(9) on one point, where he is most vulnerable, you have omitted to place your sting. I mean his palpable ignorance of the Elizabethans and many other dramatic writers of this and preceding times, with whom he ought to have formed at least a nodding acquaintance before he offered himself as physician to Melpomene.

About Shakespeare you don't say enough. He was an incarnation of nature; and you might just as well attempt to remodel the seasons, and the laws of life and death, as to alter "one jot or tittle" of his eternal thoughts. "A star" you call him. If he was a star, all the other stage scribblers can hardly be considered a constellation of brass buttons.

I say he was an universe, and all material existence with its excellences and defects was reflected in shadowy thought upon the crystal waters of his imagination, ever glorified as they were by the sleepless sun of his golden intellect. And this imaginary universe had its seasons and changes, its harmonies and its discords, as well as the dirty reality. On the snow-maned necks of its winter hurricanes rode madness, despair, and "empty death, with the winds whistling through the white grating of his sides"; its summer of poetry glistening through the drops of pity; and its solemn and melancholy autumn breathing deep melody among the "sere and yellow leaves" of thunder-stricken life, etc., etc. (See Charles Phillip's speeches and X.Y.Z. for the completing furbelow of this paragraph.)

By the third scene of the fourth act of "Macbeth," I conclude that you mean the dialogue between Malcolm and Macduff, which is only part of the scene, for the latter part, from the entrance of Rosse, is of course necessary to create an interest in the destined avenger of Duncan, as well as to set the last edge to our hatred of the usurper. The Doctor's speech is merely a compliment to the "right divine" of people in turreted night-caps to cure sores a little more expeditiously than Dr. Solomons, and is, too, a little bit of smooth chat, to show by Macduff's manner that he has not yet heard of his wife's murder.

I hope Guzman has grown since I saw him, and has improved in voice. I shall be in London in about a week, and hope to find you in your Franciscan eyrie, singing among the red-brick boughs, and laying tragedy eggs for Covent Garden Market. So you "think this last author will do something extraordinary;" so do I too. I should not at all wonder if he was to be plucked after his degree; which would be quite delightful and new.

When does Fitzgerald publish his tragedy? This March wind has blown all my sense away, and so farewell.

Ever yours,
T. L. Beddoes.

LETTER III

To Thomas Forbes Kelsall
[*Postmark "My 29, 1824"*]
6 Devereux Court
Monday 5 o clock

Dear Kelsall,—I have just arrived out of a six weeks sojourn at Bristol, and among the letters which "flake after flake had gathered" here I find yours to my absolute confusion. The very night before I went down I wrote you a long rigmaroling letter—insisting upon the necessity of 250 copies and no more being printed. In your name & Waller's I

5

had written to John Hunt giving him precisely the same information—to which he returned an answer, wh was no answer, thro' Procter. The letter containing all this and other matter I signed and sealed, but did not deliver, for I now discover that it is in my desk safely locked up & sleeping as soundly, as it's elder brother by the same pen does on Rivington's shelves. I will send it to you in envelope the first time I see a member of palavarment. What monstrous stuff that deformed Transformed is—"Rome the seven-hilly" &c

Do you think of coming to town? On the 6th of May I shall be wanting at Oxford for an examination for which I am absolutely unfit & the intervening time must be occupied in the very hardest reading. The loss of a day under such circumstances wd be a serious one but if I thought I could retrieve it at Southampton I shd be tempted to go there. If you saw a small cheap lodging in your neighbourhood, the nearer the better, and wrote by return of post I do not know what I might say. The truth is, that being a little shy & and not a little proud perhaps, I have held back & never made the first step towards discovering my residence or existence to any of my family friends—in consequence I have lived in a deserted state which I could hardly bear much longer without sinking into that despondency on the brink of which I have sate so long. Your cheerful presence at times (could we not mess together occasionally) wd set me up a good deal: but perhaps you had better not draw my heavy company on your head. I shall be obliged to read about 12 hours a day without intermission. I would not take the trouble of going down unless I was sure of seeing you a good deal; and that may be impossible.

You have caused me to write this: it means little, and you had better get out of the scrape as soon as you can—one pleasant circumstance happened to me at Bristol. I met an intelligent man who had lived at Hampstead, seen Keats, and was well read in his & the poems of Shelley. On my mentioning the former by accident to him, he complimented me on my similarity of countenance; he did not think much of K's genius & therefore did not say it insincerely or sycophantically: the same was said by Procter and Taylor before.

The Postman wait[s]
Goodnight
T. L. B.

Addressed to
  "T. F. Kelsall Esqre
    3 Houndwell Lane
      Southampton"

LETTER IV

To Thomas Forbes Kelsall
Thursday. Devx Court
1 April [1824]

Dear Kelsall,—I am sorry to find that my guardian will not let me go out of town, as he thinks my presence is necessary to the arrangement of affairs; and will be so for some weeks. I must be at Oxford on the 2nd of May, so that I fear I shall not be able to find an odd day for Southampton. From what I recollect of the enclosed letter sent exactly as I found it in my desk, there is an account of my literary proceedings, to which nothing has been added since the writing, nor will there for some time to come. I have not seen Procter yet but believe he is in town. When do you think of appearing here? You can easily manage, if your visit occurs in May, to return thro' Oxford where I shall be, quite at liberty after the first week, and at which time you will see everything to the very best advantage; much better than if you had gone there at Xmas. What sort of a letter did A. Brooke write? I am obliged to you for patching up my manners to Harrison. I saw Shelley's cousin (Mr. Shelley Harris, the greatest fool within the walls of my acquaintance) the other night at Oxford repeating the whole of the "Deformed" in raptures

God forgive him!
Yours ever—T. L. Beddoes.

Addressed
   "London, April the first 1824
    Thomas Kelsall Esqre
       Houndwell Lane
          Southampton"

"Free
Denis Gilbert"

LETTER V

To Thomas Forbes Kelsall
10 Francis Street
Tott Court Road
[*Postmark April 12 1824*]

Dear Kelsall,—Here are Beddoes & I sitting together, wondering what the devil you can have to do at Southampton during this rainy weather, that can prevent your writing a full statement of your country grievances to us, your betters, in London. You neither toil nor spin. You neither drink wine nor kiss the women. You do not read law; you do not respect religion. Friendship is a shadow with you, & Love is not even a dream.

The truth is, Mr. Thomas Kelsall, that you are fond of

your bed, of your breakfast, of reckoning up the faults of the virtuous (of us—'the few') & do not attend to the duties of your station, which are to commit your soul to paper (either in verse or prose) & send it (i.e. your soul) regularly by the Sunday's post, as an example (in one shape or another) whereby we are to avoid the evil or recreate ourselves with good. Do you go to church at Southampton? Answer, upon your oath. And, if so, is it to establish your character amongst the tea drinking dowagers there? or to entrap the heedless into a belief that you are a lawyer? Out on such doings! Do *I* go to church? Yet I have 50 times the reason that you have, for I am really an orthodox man, whereas you are little better than one of the ignorant. I stay away, to write to my friends; a duty which it seems you neglect.

You can say nothing in return, to this, under four long sides of letter paper. I feel it, & you will feel it too—& so I counsel you to begin.

Beddoes—poor Beddoes! It would hurt your feelings sadly, were you to see him. He is——but I must break it to you gently. You remember how gay he was (innocently gay) with a jibe always on his tongue, a mischievous eye, & locks curling like the hyacinth. Well what do you think has happened? He has lost—"his eye" I think I hear you say—No —not his eye. His mischievous propensities, then?—No, they are in full blossom. His innocent gaiety—No, again. He is as gay as usual, & I suppose as innocent. Why then what is the matter? Is he dead? or buried? No—he has got—"What?" (you interrupt me again)—a wife?—no, no. "A child?" no, no, no, no, I say. Why, then what, in the name of Sattan ? Why,— a wig. It is a truth, melancholy, monstrous and scarcely to be believed did not I (who am more veracious than truth itself) affirm it. "Those hanging locks" like mine or the "young Apollo's"—are clipt as close (closer than) Sampson's. Write to me soon & at length

Yours very sincerely
B. W. Procter

Dear Kelsall,—Comfort yourself with the assurance that Shelley is proceeding, and in due course of time and the Southampton coach will rise in full glory on Houndwell Lane. I can hardly write English, having bathed myself in Herodotus & Sophocles for the last fortnight; therefore I can only warn you against Procter's news; he is in an iniquitously hoaxing fit, and has resolved to take in the "countryman" with some strange story of my having a perriwig of snakes, or a lion's mane—the truth is that I have not had my head cut off as he seems to insinuate, nor am I any more like Bottom than usual. Rejoice! Baldwyn is publishing a new series of old Plays—but I forget—you prefer the fragrant pages of Lord Coke.

Yours ever
T. L. Beddoes

[The foregoing letter is written on the same sheet as that written by B. W. Procter and addressed to

Thomas Forbes Kelsaix Esqre
Houndwell Lane
Southampton]

To Thomas Forbes Kelsall
6 Devereux Court
Saturday
[*Postmark Ap: 17. 1824*]

Dear Kelsall,—I would have written before, as your letter seemed to require some sort of speedy reply, but as I was going to Mrs. Shelley's in the evening, and it was probable that some intelligence agreeable to you might be there acquired I postponed my epistolary operations. Of my visit take the result in short; the printing press moving slower than a broadwheeled waggon, only 5 proofs or 7, I forget which, yet received by Mrs. S. but she has just written a remonstrance to Hunt, and requires 5 per week. The portrait(10) not arrived—500 copies are to be printed—for 250 of which only we stand responsible—if for any, for not having received any direct answer to my communication from Hunt, I do not know whether our offer is accepted or not: and this is all I know or am likely to hear of the matter— Mr. Hogg(11) & Godwin(12) were there; the former looks and speaks like an intelligent goodnatured man, perhaps you know him; Political Justice invited me to call on him, which I intend to do, and hear what is to be heard there. Procter has been writing a catalogue raisonnie or the English Poets to accompany Baldwyn's portraits—it is just printed.
    Darley is a tallish, slender, pale, lighteyebrowed, gentle-looking, baldpate, in a brown sourtout with a duodecimo under his arm—stammering to a most provoking degree, so much so as to be almost inconversible—he is supposed to be writing a comedy & tragedy, or perhaps both in one. Mrs. Shelley has written lately in the London—a paper on ghosts in the March N° & "The Bride of Modern Italy" in the present: she has done some dramatic scenes, which P. lauds, as being very similar to Shelley's secondary style. Peacock has married a Welsh turtle,(13) and is employed at present in

11

devising inextinguishable lanterns: which he puffs at with a pair of bellows. Taylor has lately refused a paper of Procter's & one of Reynolds's,(14) & kept back Darley's reply to Terentius Secundus, for the purpose of introducing that thrice-double demoniac the economical opium-eater.(15) Exit London.

You are very unnecessarily and solicitorously suspicious of N° 1 Ancient B. Drama. Turn to your Massinger Vol 1. Preface look at the list of Plays saved from the backsides of Warburton's pies. It is out of the Lansdown collection, undoubtedly authentic, and contains some very fine things. It is to be followed by other most desirable reprints—The Devil's Law Case —Marston's Insatiate Countess—Comedies of Middleton & other previous scarcities—Moreover it is an extremely pretty little book, with a wood-cut of the Bull Theatre, and superabundantly worth the last halfcrown in your purse—you who have bought Kirk White [*word torn away*]. There was a poem of Hood's in the March New Monthly which contained P's "Michael Angelo"—H's was called The Two Ducks or swans I forget which & can say nothing about it. There is a batch of gossip for you.

Those three acts, which I cannot possibly show to any eye but that of Vulcan, are absolutely worthless, and you may imagine that I prize your good opinion too well to forfeit it knowingly. You may trust me that they are bad, if good I sh^d say so & send them, being convinced that the affectation of modesty is the hardest brass of impudence and self conceit. Be satisfied that they are damnable. There is a book of poems lately published; the author one Mr. Horace Gwynn, out of which a tasty musical dirge on Sinus was extracted in the Examiner, from this specimen I am very much inclined to augur well of the book. Procter is cooler on the subject. You tell me that Southton is not far from Oxford, I say Oxford is not far from Southton & it is much fitter for the fishingtown to come to the city & university than the contrary. Why do not you, who have all this vacant time upon you, and who could do it so much better than I or most people living, write verse yourself? If ever I sh^d become connected with a periodical, (but fear not, that is not likely:) I sh^d be sure call on you for frequent originalities & continual criticisms. For myself this—In 3 weeks time I shall set about a play, the plot of which is laid & hatched—if it is satisfactorily executed, w^h I do not expect, I shall go on; if not, "farewell the Muse" as your octave coz: w^d say

Yours ever,

T. L. B.   O tongue of women,
what a letter !

Addressed
   "Thomas F. Kelsall Esqre
     Houndwell Lane
      Southampton"

"Single"

LETTER VII

To Bryan Waller Procter
Milan, June 8th [1824]

Dear Procter,—If I do not dream, this is the city of Sforza, and today I have seen a picture of his wife by Leonardo da Vinci. Paris, Lyons, Turin and Novara, and beautiful Chambéry in its bed of vines, they have passed before me like the Drury Lane Diorama, and I almost doubt whether I have been sitting in the second tier or on the top of the diligence.

Paris is far preferable to London as a place of amusement, and the manner of the lower orders is strikingly superior to that of their island equals. I saw the opera; the ballet much better than ours, but the music was French: the house is not

13

nearly so commodious or elegant as Drury Lane, and the painting and mechanism of their scenery is not so dexterous and brilliant. The Teatro della Scala in this city I have not yet seen; it is considered only inferior to the San Carlo at Naples. Savoy, from the French frontier to Chambéry, is the most beautiful country I have yet seen; nothing between the Alps and Milan is equally rich, varied, and delightful. Towards the Alps the vines grow thinner, and give place at first to corn, then to ragged herbage, and finally mother earth hides her head under a coverlid of snow; and with their country and climate change the inhabitants. You have the goitred and the crétins instead of the Savoyard of gentle manners and frank countenance. On the frontiers of fertile Italy they brought us a salad of dandelions at dinner.

June 9th.—Since I began this letter I have been to the top of the cathedral, and in the pit of the Teatro della Scala. The former is the finest church externally which I have seen; but the interior of Westminster's old Abbey is triumphant over the marble simplicity of the Milanese's concave. The roof is finished with pinnacles and battlements of white marble of a workmanship as exquisite as if it were in ivory. From the summit, all the rich country from Alp to Apennine, river and hill and wood, the cool lakes and the vineyards of an ardent green, lay themselves at your feet.

Last night the clouds had unrolled from the mountains, which were themselves as visionary as clouds; the "roof of blue Italian weather" was here and there decorated by a tapestried vapour, silver or pale gold, gathered up among the stars and slowly toiling along the calm air. The sun fell quietly behind the Alps, and the moment he touched them, it appeared that all the snows took fire and burned with a candescent brilliancy. (I hope you like the opening of my new novel, as contained in the preceding paragraph.)

Now for Delia Scala. It is avast theatre —six tiers of boxes, all hung with silk, disposed like our window curtains, of a light blue or yellow colour, the pit, I should think, almost twice as large as Covent Garden's. The opera was "Tancredi." Madame Sesta the prima donna, old, but generally preferred to Pasta; the primo basso, a most extraordinary singer, with tones more like those of an organ than any human creature. The scenery is not, in my opinion, equal to the best at our theatres. One of the drops was a sort of Flemish painting; the subject, a village carnival, very well executed. Such a thing would be novel at C. G. if it could be well, but it must be very well, done. Now that silk is so cheap, too, I think they might be a little more lavish of draperies; but we are not managers yet. The ballet, *i baccanali aboliti*, incalculably superior to ours or the French in the exquisite grace of the grouping, the countless abundance of dancers, and the splendour and truth of costume and decoration. The house was about one-third full, and the people all talking; so that there was a buzz—outbuzzing the Royal Exchange—all the night except during "Di tanti palpiti."

And what else have I seen? A beautiful and far-famed insect—do not mistake, I mean neither the Emperor, nor the King of Sardinia, but a much finer specimen—the firefly. Their bright light is evanescent, and alternates with the darkness, as if the swift wheeling of the earth struck fire out of the black atmosphere; as if the winds were being set upon this planetary grindstone, and gave out such momentary sparks from their edges. Their silence is more striking than their flashes, for sudden phenomena are almost invariably attended with some noise, but these little jewels dart along the dark as softly as butterflies. For their light, it is not nearly so beautiful and poetical as our still companion of the dew—the glow-worm with his drop of moonlight. If you see or write to Kelsall, remember me to him; and excuse my neglect in not writing to him before I left England by the plea of hurry, which is true. To-night at twelve I leave Milan, and shall be at Florence on Saturday long before this letter tastes the atmosphere (*pardonnez*, I mean the smoke) of London.

> There and here,
> Yours truly,
> T. L. Beddoes.

If you see Mrs. Shelley, ask her to remember me, and tell her that I am as anxious to change countries with her as she can be. If I could be of any use in bringing the portrait, etc., it would be a proud task, but most likely I only flash over Florence; entering on the flood of the stars, and departing with their ebb.

LETTER VIII

To Thomas Forbes Kelsall
6 Devereux C Temple Bar.
[Postmark Au: 25 1824]

Dear Kelsall,—I should have written to you some time ago if I had not hoped to see you before this: some business will detain me in town ten days or perhaps a fortnight longer—at the expiration of which I hope to have a month or so for Southampton. Tho' I depend very little on my poetical faculty, it is my intention to complete one more tragedy, on the comparative merits or demerits of which future determinations will depend.

The disappearance of Shelley from the world, seems, like the tropical setting of that luminary (*aside* I hate that word) to which his poetical genius can alone be compared with reference to the companions of his day, to have been followed by instant darkness and owl-season; whether the vociferous Darley is to be the comet, or tender fullfaced L. E. L. the milk-and-watery moon of our darkness, are questions for the astrologers: if I were the literary weather-guesser for 1825 I would safely prognosticate fog, rain, blight in due succession for it's dullard months—But I beg your pardon, this was all said forgetting your relation to the eternal Gerard —By the way I was two days at Canterbury, and did not see your correspondent Arthur—What an omission! But I saw

Savagius at Florence. You have read his book and think something of him by this time.

And are you cricketting? N. or M. Who gave you that Ball? &c How did you like the Effigies Poeticæ? And the Second Maiden?(16) Verily that is worth the whole heap of Horace Gwynn, L. E. L., Midsummer day dreams, and Bernard-bartonizings of this years press. The arrogance and conceit of your cousin's connections appears to me utterly insufferable and disgusting; and the increase of that pernicious Blackwood system—particularly among these younger men, is the very worst sign of their mind & public imbecillity. I would greatly prefer the return of the old dull prosing times, when every author was "the ingenious" and his miscellany "excellent" at the top of an acrostic; even Johnson's very unbearable and absurd self was less mischievous. But I won't despond, for I wish to cry at Walker's next Trag.(5)

I was very much pleased to hear of Mrs. Shelley's arrangement with old Timothy(17) and to see the very great alteration for the better and the happier in her appearance and manner. She is writing something. Procter is idle of course—no I beg his pardon, he's been 10 miles out of town this week. And now, being sleepy and stupid, I wish you goodnight.

Yours ever
T. L. Beddoes

P.S. Shelley's book—This is a ghost indeed, and one who will answer to our demand for hidden treasure. The Dirge for the Year—That Indian fragment—The boat on the Serchio and the Letter—with Music are to me the best of the new things and perfectly worthy of the mind which produced them. The translation of Mercury's hymn too; though questionable as to the fidelity of it's tone, is delightfully easy —

What would he not have done, if ten years more, that will be wasted upon the lives of unprofitable knaves and fools, had been given to him. Was it that more of the beautiful and good, than Nature could spare to one, was incarnate in him, and that it was necessary to resume it for distribution through the external and internal worlds? How many springs will blossom with his thoughts—how many fair and glorious creations be born of his one extinction.

Addressed to
"Thomas Kelsall Esq.
Houndwell Lane 3
Southampton"

LETTER IX

To Thomas Forbes Kelsall
6 D[*evereux*] Court
Monday
[*Postmark Oct: 4, 1824*]

Dear Kelsall,—A letter according to your desire, which I foresee will be full of emptiness—in the first place to say that I must stay in town till the beginning of next month and how much longer depends upon the operations of the Court of Chancery and its' Lord—if any letter should stray into your Lodgings, be so good as to forward it hither; as for the other chattels, unless they grow too large for your harbouring, you will, I dare say, let them remain till I can come for them.

I have seen Procter once, he was then at the Prince of Wales's, but he has now left that and Francis St.; for what bower, cave, or Attic I am ignorant. I gave him your command to visit or write; therefore I may conclude that he has not done either—Nothing of any interest in town except a couple of live crocodiles in St. Martin's Lane, and an excessive clever new comic actress, who has twice appeared

18

at the Haymarket. Meantime, o base Southampton, what have you done to Miss Tree? Should not your theatre in Mercy be burnt, and Shalders & his gang be hung, like a necklace of rats, upon one string—? You see that poor Maturin(18) is ill; not dangerously I hope, for we can hardly spare so much talent in our present poverty. By Blackwood's advertisement I observe a letter to Procter, an insult of course. The London condescends to a vast deal of scandal and idle chat about the "noble bard." What say you to these lines?

> *A comely knight, all armed*
> *Thro' whose bright ventail lifted up on high*
>   *His manly face*
> *Looked forth, as Phœbus, face out of the East*
> *Betwixt two shady mountains doth arise—*

Whose can they be ?

I have not done much in German, just tasted the nouns but not touched the verbs—in fact it is a feast at which I strictly obey the innkeepers law—eat what you can, but pocket none—How do you like O'Connor? You'll not be surprised to hear that I have begun and nearly finished another, a new 1st Act—and am quite tired of it. P[*rocter*] hopes that he'll be able to finish an alteration of Lee's Duke of Guise for C Kemble this season—they talk of a new comedy by Croly(19)—further knoweth not

Yours sincerely

T. L. B.

read the 12th Canto Book II of the Faerie Queen. Canto 6 Book III. and a noble stanza LIV. Canto XI. Book I. "So down he fell" &c which ought to be added to Coleridge's note on Deborah's Song—

LETTER X

> *To* Thomas Forbes Kelsall
> *26 Mall*
> *Clifton*
> *Bristol*
> [*Postmark Nov: 8. 1824*]

What the fifteen hundred devils can have become of that fellow Beddoes? Why here he is on a wet sunday morning at Clifton, a bad pen and nothing to say, being prosperous auspices for the beginning of a letter. Perhaps you thought that I was delaying till I could epistolize in German—but in truth that tongue has flooded my brain no higher than der die das.

One morning at Procter's just after breakfast came a letter from Southton which touched my letterwriting conscience to the quick: it recounted your jaundice, but that I trust is, like Mathew's little pig, all over—and you are reinstated on the sofa in H Lane, where November darkens & clients to come cast their shadows before. Believe me I have begun two letters before, written a page of each and torn them up in despair of finishing. This however I will end.

I have seen Procter, before I left London, once or twice when his honeymoon was reduced to a cheese-paring—though he is now only half of himself he is twice the man he was, and I do not think that you will not be disappointed with his tenderer moiety. He is intending to give Covent Garden Lee's altered play this season & altogether appears very industriously inclined: this is as it should be: he has

20

open sea enough if he will but take the tide.

I have been turning over old plays in the Brit: Museum; and verily think that another volume of specimens might be very well compiled—when I go up again, perhaps I shall do it for my private use. I was very much disappointed with the dulness that hid itself under the alluring title, which you must often have admired; to wit: See me and see me not, or Hans Beerpots invisible comedy.(30) Marston's Sophonisba contains very good things and there are some very smart and quaintly worded speeches & characters in some of Middleton's comedys; the dullest thing possible is the Birth of Merlin, ascribed to W. Shakspeare: if Steam engines shall ever write blank verse it will be such as that:

Excuse me for a little bit of remonstrance. I do not think you were born to be confined to sheep's skins, you should spread a sense of true criticism, if you are disinclined to set an example in another way; crush Campbell(21) throw Bowles(22) into the fire, Bernard & such small beer into the pig's trough.

Farewell, this is a stunted communication but I am dull & en veritè hurried

Yours ever
T. L. Beddoes

The four first acts of the fatal Dowry(38) have improved my opinion of Massinger; he is a very effective "stage-poet" after all. I have not forgotten that I owe you five shillings and a multitude of dinners—if you do not go to London to receive them, I shall honestly do it at Southton before long.

Addressed to
"T. F. Kelsall Esqre
3 Houndwell Lane
Southampton"

To Thomas Forbes Kelsall
Clifton Dec 6 [1824]

Dear Kelsall,—I shall not fail you in London, tho' the time is but ill defined by 'Christmas', which in vulgar acceptation may shadow forth some week or fortnight from the 25th Dec inclusive. I take it for granted that you are one of those comfortable mortals, who have fire places with open arms & expecting arm-chairs to embrace them at whatever town they visit; otherwise for quiet, attention, & economy I could recommend 6 D. Court, where a bed room, with or without sitting room, is to be had by the night or week. (You see when I have worn out my wings I shall make a very passable and praiseworthy advertisement-writer.)

I shall be there however if not before, immediately after the day after carols & mincepies. Meantime lost to all German and all humane learning, o'erhusked with sweet dozing sloth, writing now and then some such an unsightly scrawl as this, or scratching a tuneless and abortive verse, I ensconce myself in the hospitality of my Clifton demi-uncle. He is a man worthy of no slight mention, connected to me slightly by marriage with my mother's sister.

Born in the town of Berne, bred in Germany, a fugitive from his relations & theology, he left behind him a fair Swiss fortune in hand, & Church dignity had he but stepped in the shoes of Jack Calvin, & submitted quietly his shoulders & belief to the Geneva gown. This not being his will, he shipped himself for England & began his London existence as an engraver & painter. This failed, and after making literary proposals, which were coldly received by the booksellers of that unGermanized time, he took to surgery & came to Bristol, in the democratic dawn of Southey, Coleridge &c. To the former he was closely attached, corresponded & hexameterized with him—made acquaintance with Davy, the opium-eater, my father, & all that was then—& might, had

22

not a fatal democratic boldness & ecclesiastical antipathy barred his ascent, have been one of the most opulent & celebrated, as he is confessedly one of the best, living surgeons. But this is not all: to the dead he adds a radical acquaintance with the living tongues of Europe, an intimacy with the practice & theory of the pictorial art, & an inexhaustible fund of literary knowledge, German & English being both his native tongues. This is nothing higher than the truth, & yet his name is quite unknown out of the circle of his present & former professions.

O ghost of butcher-basket-born Kirke White! hast thou read the last London & its proposal of geminating its monthly birth—anticipation of much lead. Yet were I P[*rocter*] I would rather lend it a shoulder than Colburn's. But I asked you whether you had seen it, because it contains a review of Darley's first English product—his Exstatic Errors —which, from the extracts, I should say was more talented and rich in indication of good than what he has since done. How he will be hunted & abused when he appears in *propria*, for the rudeness & arrogance of John Lacy! A new tragic abortion of mine has absolutely extended its fœtus to a quarter of the fourth act: when finished—if finished—I think it will satisfy you and myself of my poetical and dramatic impotence . . . The mystery, you see, is torn from Ravenna; which, if it persists, in spite of, the dramatic calvinism of the pit, in being alive when it ought to be damned, we'll see. And so good night—

Yours truly
T. L. Beddoes

Addressed to
> "T. F. Kelsall Esq
> Houndwell Lane 3
> Southampton"

("The original of this letter given by me to Miss King, Nov. 1852—the daughter of his demi-uncle." *Endorsement by Kelsall*.)

To Thom*as Forbes Kelsall*
26 Mall. Clifton
[*Postmark Jan 11, 1925*]

Dear Kelsall,—Day after day since Xmas I have intended
to write or go to London & day after day I have deferred both
projects—and now—I will give you the adventures and
mishaps of this present sunday. Remorse, and startling
conscience, in the form of an old sulky & a shying horse,
hurried me to the Regulator coach-office on Saturday—"Does
the regulator & its team conform to the Mosaic decalogue,
Mr. Book-keeper?" He broke Priscian's head & thro' the
aperture assured me that it did not—I was booked for the
inside—call at 26 Mall for me—"Yes sir at ½ p. 5 am."—at 5 I
rose like a ghost from the tomb & betook me to coffee. No
wheels rolled through the streets but the inaudible ones of
that uncreated hour—It struck 6—a coach was called—we
hurried to the office but the coach was gone—here followed a
long Brutus & Cassius discourse between a shilling-buttoned
waist-coatteer of a porter and myself—which ended in my
extending mercy to the suppliant coach-owners —& agreeing
to accept a place for Monday—

All well thus far. The Biped knock of the post alighted on
the door at 12—& two letters were placed upon my german
dictionary—Your own—which I at first intended to reply to
vivã voce—had not the second informed [*me*] of my brother's
arrival in England, his short leave of absence, & his intention
to visit me here next week. This twisted my strong purpose
like a thread,—and disposed me to remain here about 10
days further. On the 21st at latest I go to London. Be there & I
will join you, or if not pursue you to Southampton.

The fatal dowry(23) has been cobbled sure, by some
purblind ultracrepidarian. McReady's friend Walker very
likely—but nevertheless I maintain 'tis a good play—& might
have been rendered very effective—by docking it of the whole

24

fifth Act which is an excrescence—re-creating Novall—& making Beaumelle a good deal more ghost-gaping & moonlightish—The cur: tailor has taken out the most purple piece in the whole weft—the end of the 4th act—& shouldered himself into toleration thro' the prejudices of the pit, when he should have built his admiration on their necks.

Say what you will—I am convinced the man who is to awaken the drama must be a bold trampling fellow—no creeper into worm-holes—no reviser even—however good. These reanimations are vampire-cold—Such ghosts as Marloe—Webster &c are better dramatists, better poets, I dare say, than any contemporary of ours—but they are ghosts —the worm is in their pages—& we want to see something that our great-grandsires did not know. With the greatest reverence for all the antiquities of the drama I still think, that we had better beget than revive—attempt to give the literature of this age an idiosyncrasy & spirit of its own & only raise a ghost to gaze on not to live with—just now the drama is a haunted ruin.

I am glad that you are awakening to a sense of Darley—he must have no little perseverance to have gone thro so much of that play—it will perchance be the first star of a new day. Remember me to Procter & reproach him for his idleness to the fullest extent of vituperative civility—if I could find a reproof as heavy as the new London Mag I'd hurl it on him—I have written a new plot—& forgotten it. Will Keene (?) anatomize Mr. T. Campbell? even after

> *But, reaching home, terrific omen! There*
> *The straw-laid street preluded his despair—*
> *The servants' look: the table that revealed*
> *His letter sent to Charlotte last still sealed—&c*

Theodoric

Stay in town if you can.
Yours truly
T. L. Beddoes

25

LETTER XIII

> *To* Thomas Forbes Kelsall
> *14 Southampton Row*
> *Friday Morning*
> [*Postmark 25 March 1925*]

Dear Kelsall,—As Beddoes has offered me the use of part of his frank, I am desirous of taking advantage of it so far as to enable me to acknowledge the receipt of your letter—which I hereby do accordingly. I will endeavour shortly to answer it, but not to answer it shortly. I shall be infinitely amusing & not inconsiderably dextrous, & so I give thee warning.—Touching myself and my pursuits, I have been for some time on the sort of thing you hint at, & have done, what I have done, better than I was afraid I could. You shall see something by the time you & June come together to Southampton, both of you in flower while I am in fruit. Tell me—or rather my wife (who makes this enquiry, while she desires her best remembrances to you) when we may expect you in London—& whether it is to be for 2 months or for 3? My tragedy(24) goes on slowly—a poor dozen lines, or fragment of speech now & then, but what has been added is in my 'best manner'—as they take [?] of Raffaelle & such folks.

Of Beddoes I will give you no account. Let him speak for himself, & say why he has not done anything lately. I can give no reason for it, unless it be that he idles over Greek and

26

German, & leave[s] the English Parnassus for the Transalpine & transmarine places. I reserve my news for a future sheet of paper. You shall have everything down to the advertisements—What should you say if you were to see me some green morning (or evening) stepping out of the Southampton 'Intelligence' with a bundle of MS under one arm & my portmantel under the other? You, who are a believer in ghosts, would go home & secure your mutton chop with out delay, of course; knowing what a chamelion from the other world would do if he came suddenly upon the eatables of this. But, be easy. I am long time projecting you know, although I am so rapid in my executions. You may therefore sleep quietly on your straw for this fortnight to come, if conscience & the warm weather will permit it.

Have you read the 'Odes & Addresses to Great People'? (25)—It is a joint production by that united Beaumont & Fletcher brotherhood—Reynolds & Hood. What a pity it is that Hood should have given up serious poetry for the sake of cracking the shells of jokes which have not always a kernel! But Adieu! I leave the rest of this virgin sheet for Beddoes's eloquence to stir itself—& you. He says that he shall be lively beyond measure & give you part of his reason in rhyme

Yours ever
B. W. Procter

My dear Kelsall,—After a long & shameful period of silence I venture to address you, having got Procter to break the ice of this frank. I will leave out all explanations, excuses & apologies—painful & unnecessary things—& go straight to the communication of such stuff as my brain entertains this morning. In the first place, lo! I am expert in reading German, even so far as now to be employing an hour a day or so in the metrical translation of the old obscure tedious Nibelungen-lied—about 100 lines is all as yet finished of this work—a grain from the mountain of 9560 of w^h it is compact.

As usual I have begun a new tragedy w^h at present I think of completing. I understand that Mr. Thomas Campbell has in some newspaper in a paltry refutation of some paltry charge of plagiarism regarding his paltry poem in the paltry Edinburgh touched the egg of my last man—the gentleman is completely addled, & the steam of my teapot will never be powerful enough to supply the place of incubation; nevertheless sometime or other I will treat it, not in the style of Hopkins & Campbell.

You have seen or heard of the Oxford Magazine—I am told that it is the progeny of my college and one or two others —it's best & principal contributor in the *Praed*(26) line being one ingenious Mr White, a clever youth who is my successor in the literary chair at Pembroke. They have dunned me for a contribution & tho' I anticipate precocious dullness & an early death I believe I shall be foolish enough to write them some special bad rhymes—sh^d you think of going on with German I can get you a book or two very cheap—e.g. Schiller's Gedichte—bound (if they are not sold) the best edition 7/6. Bohte selling it in it's unwedded sheets for 14^8—I have two or three odd volumes of *works* but complete as *poems*, w^h I will save you too if you speak. Learn it by all means—it's literature touches the heaven of the Greek in many places—& the language is as easy as possible, to my notion more so than French—I have been seriously studying it since New Year's day only—& can read Schiller with little difficulty—Goethe in his poems &c unvulgarised & cantstuffed writings easily—Noëhdens dict^y the best little one —if you are discontented with your own, is to be had cheaply I know where—

For many reasons at this moment it is impossible to Southamptonise—I must soon go to Ireland. At Present the law is on me—you know what a beast it is, & after my return from the Emerald mother of potatoes I shall have to settle my sisters, settle my affairs, sell & pay & impoverish myself to the bone & then set off for Germany; but be sure I do not leave England without seeing you, nor, if I can but finish, without dropping into the press some frail memorial of my existence—

The state of literature now is painful & humiliating enough—every one will write for £15 a sheet—who for love of art, who for fame, who for the purpose of continuing the noble stream of English minds? We ought too to look back with late repentance & remorse on our intoxicated praise, now cooling, of Lord Byron—such a man to be so spoken of when the world possessed Goëthe, Schiller, Shelley!

Oh self satisfied England—this comes of Always looking at herself in the looking glass of the sea, I suppose.

Adio

T. L. B
6 Devereux C^t

Addressed to
"London March the twenty fifth 1825
    Thomas Kelsall Esqre
      Houndwell Lane
       Southampton"

Free
    Denis Gilbert

Not quite so much as you deserve, my dear Kelsall, not quite a quire of spoiled paper accompanies this. I believe the valuable autumn-hued envelope is the most deserving of the collection—read if you can—& the Lord have mercy on you & pardon your wilfulness. I cannot find your larking cloud song, I daresay it is in my desk w^h is apud te in Houndwell lane—but I wrote in the coach w^h brought me from Southampton to London 5 months since—a famous one beginning—

Ho! Adam the carrion crow
The old crow of Cairo &c

w^h is sung with much applause by one of my dramatis personae in the unfinished drama No. 3 in my possession. Procter saw the enclosed sheets & pretended to have read them but I thought he looked as if he was talking loud only & did not believe him.

I am clear of the Oxford, but have been dunned for No. 2 & as I shall very likely be there in a week or so—I shall give 'em some such stuff as Netley Abbey—w^h I turned up in looking for the canine cloud—because I want to get a criticism w^h I have just begun on Montezuma—a thing I like vastly, to be printed—& hope they'll be bribed by my rhyme to swallow my reason—& there is an excellent sonnet of mine to a terrier whose biography & portrait I will append pathetically. I have not sent you Schiller's Gedichte: because there is an edition of his whole work Taschen-buch size, that is like your stupid Herman & Dorothea but printed in a real and very good German type—w^h is printing by subscription for £1. 16. 0. 12 vols are out, there are to be 20—& you will receive them safely—this is what I recommend.

All that one hears of Schiller inclines one to admire him much more than his fat, leather-chopped, fish-eyed rival with the mock star of Vonity on his padded coat. I have read that fellow's Tasso w^h is a disgraceful apology for the conduct of the Duke of Ferrara, & represents poor Torquato, who was no great wit I fear, as an absolute spoiled poetic madman, a sort of Italian Tom Campbell—as touchy as tinder and as valuable. This was bound in a volume with his Iphigenie in Tauris, a poem faultlessly delightful, unless it be a fault that instead of being an imitation of Euripides it is a victory over him. I never felt so much disgust or much more admiration for any poet than for this Goëthe, as I read thro' it—& I believe every one who reads all his works must have this double feeling of contempt of & delight in him—both nearly measureless—but he has no principle; in thinking of Schiller you have more to admire than the paper he has written on.

The metrical translation I was rash enough to speak about stands thus—

you see why I don't send it. It is waiting to be finished—
meantime I have abandoned my last new act—& begun the
3rd of that w^h I was writing at Southton I believe I may make
an end of one or two in this way—

Be so good as to read—(if you can or do intend it) with a
pencil in your hand & scratch all that is more particularly
detestable & bad than ye rest.

Yours

T. L. B.

I send you an easy little poem of Wieland's it is complete
in itself. The best of rhyme is that it teaches pronunciation.

Avoid Noehden in this particular he tells you to pronounce ů & aů oi—ei—or ī is the right thing but I suppose his
friend Dr. Stoddart (in partnership with whom he
perpetrated that vile translation of Don Carlos you boast of
behind your law-books) is Worcestershire and says bile—ile
—tile &c as bad rhymers do instead of boil oil & even to think
of w^h makes ones blood crawl as if there were spiders in the
veins—Bohte is publishing a catalogue with preface by A. W.
Schlegel—& when you are German in every pore, as you will
want some, apply for them to the man whose card I enclose
—he has a small collection of second-hand Germanities &
will get them for you new at a discount of 12 per cent (ready
money new English books the same.)

I have most completely mastered the art of living in
London & can hardly bring myself to leave it it is so cheap—
Antrobus & Co. Teamen nearly opposite Northumber land St.
Strand sell some of the best black tea I ever tasted for 6^8 a
pound put a piece of lemon-peel into your pot & it gives the
flavour of green—(a fee for that) All we invalids take a piece
of broiled bacon with our breakfast each morn, try it (ditto)

T.L. B

31

I will do the last man before I die but it is a subject I save up for a time when I have more knowledge, a freer pencil, a little menschen-lehre, a command of harmony & an accumulation of picturesque ideas, & dramatic characters fit for the theme. Meantime let Tom Campbell rule his roast & mortify the ghost of Sternhold—it is a subject for Michael Angelo not for the painter of Admiral Granby on the sign post. Did I tell ye, I had a very dull interview with that dealer in broken English, Dr. Spurzheim, the ambassador from Golgotha? he is a strange breeches-full of mankind & seems inclined to the asinine.

Procter is—Oh I mustn't tell, if you don't choose to buy Schillers Sämmtliche Werke w^h I mention, I have an odd vol of Schiller's Gedichte much at your service. Bohte, has the other but the Jew wants 7^8 for it —they fit very well.

Addressed to
T. F. Kelsall Esqre

LETTER XIV

To Thomas Forbes Kelsall
Pemb: Coll.
Oxford
[*Postmark 14 Ap 1825*]

My dear Kelsall,—If you have no inclination to insert yourself in the Oxford coach w^h: passes by the top of Houndwell St at 8 each morning, w^h I think you could do as easily as visit Fareham. I will thank you if you will pick the lock of my trunk put all the books &c into it & send it to me here as soon as convenient. I hope you have been very dull and tired with the MSS I sent you, headache and hypochondria were what you deserved for snapping the thread w^h suspended such a weight of lead above your unhappy and now suffering brainpan.

I left Procter writing, more for the Edinburgh, New Monthly, & retrospective, I fear, than for the drama; he is locked up every morning from 10 till ½ p. 1 by his wife with ½ a quire of foolscap & a quill—Why did you not, when last in town, pay your respects to Mrs. Shelley at Kentish town? I saw the other day, very well, & enjoying the Italian April, Mr. White, who, I find, is in very low repute here just at present, [*he*] has been writing an obliging continuation of Don Juan— to moralize the noble Spaniard. Knight is going to resuscitate his magazine, excluding original poetry entirely, what will cousin Moultrie(27) say? Mr. Praed has lately become a private tutor at Eton; this has chagrined all his poetical friends exceedingly. Pray do not attribute any of the Oxford Magazine to me; but come up here as soon as you can—& bring my things with you, all turned into the trunk if possible —have no mercy on the lock; it is a vile one.

Yours truly
T. L. Beddoes

Addressed to
"T. F. Kelsall Esqre
   3 Houndwell Lane
    Southampton

LETTER XV

To Thomas Forbes Kelsall
Pemb Coll
Oxford Wednesday
[*Postmark 8 Ju: 1825*]

Yet once more O thou Kelsall yet once more I bestow on you a chance of investigating Alfred's university. On Wednesday next is the commemoration, a high and solemn act of academic mummery at w[h] Chantrey(28) is to receive a degree of LLD—I therefore recommend you to take a place on the roof of the Southton on Monday morn[g] you will get here by dinner time—Tuesday will be consumed in seeing leonine wonders, Wednesday you shall go to the theatre, & (if so inclined) hear the spouting of prize verses &c—& in the eve[g] a concert—on Thursday then you may rush back to your sheepskins in the Lane—Besides here is another attraction w[h] I had well nigh forgotten, the new N° of the Oxford Quarterly is to be produced on the occasion, in w[h] there will be a translation of a very curious high German piece of Schiller's called the "Philosophische Briefe"—executed by your obedient servant—

Oxford is the most indolent place on earth—I have fairly done nothing in the world but read a play or two of Schiller, Æschylus, & Euripides—you I suppose read German now as fast as English—There is a cheap copy of Schiller's Drama to be had in Tottenham Court Road—about 1£. w[h] I shall be happy to get on commission as I go to town next week.

I do not intend to finish that 2nd Brother you saw but am thinking of a very Gothic-styled tragedy for w[h] I have a jewel of a name—

Death's Jestbook—of course no one will ever read it—Mr. Milman (our poetry professor) has made me quite unfashionable here by denouncing me, as one of a "villainous school." I wish him another son—

Oxford idleness the heat of the day, & the clock w[h] is just striking the hour for my lecture on Comparative anatomy break me off—Let me see you on Monday or Tuesday—the former day I recommend as it will give you an opportunity of seeing the last boat race this season

Yours ever
T. L. Beddoes

Addressed to
    "T. F. Kelsall Esqre
      3 Houndwell Lane
        Southampton"

LETTER XVI

To Thomas Forbes Kelsall
Hamburg
Tuesday, 19. July 1825

My dear Kelsall,—und mein lieber herr Thomas,—If you will take the sails of the Harwich packet, walk across the German Ocean, trot up the Elbe, & turn into the Roman Emperor at Hamburg be so good as to enquire for mein Herr T. L. B. No 12 up two pair of stairs, & you will find him sitting on a horse-hair sofa, looking over the Elbe with his meerschaum at his side full of Grave & abundantly prosaic.

Tomorrow, according to the prophecies of the diligence he will set out for Hanovver (we Germans (here a puff.) always spell it with 2v's—) & by the end of this week mein Herr Thomas will probably be a Dr of the university of Göttingen. What his intentions further may be I cannot say precisely as you & I between ourselves recollect that he is not altogether endued with the polar virtue of perseverance, &

35

that the needle with w^h he embroiders his cloth of life has not been rubbed with the magnet of steady determination. I rather think however that he will return to England with a rather quaint and unintelligible tragedy, which will set all critical pens nib upwards, a la fretful porcupine.

When he embarked from Harwich & observed that his only companions were two Oxford men, professors of *genteel larking*, without the depth, vivacity or heartiness w^h is necessary to render such people tolerable, he instantly drew his shell over him, & remained impenetrably proud & silent every wave of the way, dropping now and then a little venom into the mixture of conversation to make it effervesce.

Hamburg, where he now is, poor young man, is a new brick built town a fit place to embellish the ugly genius of the broad flat sided muddy Elbe—The very churches of brick & emetical unto the eye—The people honest and civil, & God fill their purse for it, no custom house no passport required— but then the women are of a coarse quality—there are no pictures no sculpture & if one meets more upright & manly forms in life, than in Italy, yet you seek in vain paintings superior to signs or sculpture beyond a tobacco-stopper.

Herr Procter, the Boet as George the Second says, will tell you what a confusion was caused by your hoaxing letter to a B. A of Pemb. Coll. Oxon—what a scrawl it ilicited from his drowsy quill & how *underlined* was the reply. Now leb wohl —for the post leaves us soon.

Fahrend oder reitend
sein
Der Genius von T. L. B

[*Addressed to*]
    "T. F. Kelsall Esqre
      3 Houndwell Lane
       Southampton
       England

To Thomas Forbes Kelsall
Cassel. Sept 29 [1925]

Dear Kelsall,—If you ever received a shabby small letter from Hamburg you know that I am a Göttingen student; it is likely that I shall remain so for some time. This university is a handsome likeness of the caricature given of it in all works of the day which exhibit Germany to the delight of you people in that island, but if there is more harm, I believe there is also more good in it than in our own.

Blumenbach(29) who is my best friend among the professors, is I fancy of the first rank as mineralogist, phisologian, geologist, botanist, natural historian & physician, over and above which he possesses an exuberant fancy & a flow of wit w^h is anything but German; indeed I suspect that he is the first living writer in Deutschland, for a nearer acquaintance with Goethe has inclined me to rate him much lower than I had anticipated; out of his works w^h fill pretty fatly some 30 vols—not like Mr. Colburns in capacity of page—3 at most contain what is really good. As a poet is he inferior to his late lordship(30) and in the novel line somewhere about Mackenzie. The hasty Germans have betrayed their literature & delivered it to the enemy by exalting him to the supreme godship thereof—but ere his bones are cool probably they will pull down his statue from it's high pinnacle on the poetic temple and make it a step to the high altar of some new pen-deity—

They treat their poets as the Romans did their emperors —alive they are golden heavenly fellows for whom reviews ascend like triumphal arches—they die a weeping willow & an elegy stick over their graves, and as the tree draws nourishment out of their decaying corporeal substance, a younger rival sets the roots of his fame in their literary remains and flourishes as fast as these latter rot; so Goethe has done with regard to Klopstock & Wieland. Their follies

37

about his sitting between Shakespeare & Sophocles are laughed at every where but in the university—pothouses when they grow glorious on the fumes of smallest ale & rankest tobacco: Nevertheless learn your German if you are not already master of it, as I suppose: for the solider literature deserves it—History I mean & criticism of the true sort—

Ludwig Tieck is just about to publish in English & German a number of the Elizabethan fellows—the young folk will then become acquainted with our literary commoners, the steps up to Shakespeare, & if they do not grow giddy on the ascent will have an opportunity of contemplating from the sides & terraces of this mountainous poetry the molehill w^h Goethe & Schiller have thrown up & called the German Parnasso—

I am preparing for deep & thorough medical studies: for I find literary wishes fading pretty fast—however I have writ two acts of an affair w^h if ever consummated will be tolerably decent—better I hope than Campbell &c I gave the thing I sent you about Pygmalion(31) to the poor Oxford magaziners but don't know whether they ever intended to print it—No one will read it if they do for their pages are the shortest cut to oblivion one can think of. And now how do you get on in England: has cousin John(32) calved any more Epicisms? Have Darley, C. Lamb, Mrs. Shelley &c printed? In a word have you anything worth reading? or that you can read without many struggles?

I am here at Cassel a pretty little Capital of a pretty great rascal, the Elector of Cassel, whose father sold some thousands of his wretched subjects to England that he might expend the price of their heads in making a fine garden & building a palace in w^h he can't live. You see what sort of letters I write, & you may bless your stars that they are only quarterly apparitions—I am going to write to Procter just such another, so you may comfort yourself with the thought that there's fellowship in your post-office misery—

Whenever your pen is unemployed on sheepskins favour me with a line addressed to Herr B—bey Keil. Juden Strasse. Göttingen—Hannover. There are two of the great Rothschild's sons studying here just opposite me. At Leipsic they have printed a Shakspeare in one vol. very decently & the first edit, of Hamlet. Noehden is right as to the pronunciation of eu—it is *oi*—& a very broad one too in Hannover where they speak German best.

T. L. B

Addressed to
"T. F. Kelsall Esqre
3 Houndwell Lane
Southampton
Engelland"

Single
Oct 4

LETTER XVIII

To Thomas Forbes Kelsall
Postmark
Gottingen Decr 4 [1825]
Sunday

My dear Kelsall,—Up at 5 Anatomical reading till 6—translation from English into German till 7—Prepare for Blumenbach's lecture on comp. Anat^y & breakfast till 8—Blumenbach's lecture till 9—Stromeyer's(33) lecture on

Chemistry till 10. 10 to ½ p. 12. Practical Zootomy—½ p. 12 to 1 English into German or German literary reading with a pipe—1 to 2 Anatomical lecture. 2 to 3 anatomical reading. 3 to 4 Osteology. 4 to 5 Lecture in German language. 5 to 6 dinner and *light* reading in Zootomy, Chem. or Anat^y. 6 to 7 this hour is very often wasted in a visit sometimes Anatomical reading till 8. Then coffee and read Greek till 10. 10 to 11. write a little Death's Jest book w^h is a horrible waste of time, but one must now & then throw away the dregs of the day; read Latin sometimes or even continue the Anatomy —and at 11 go to bed.

I give you this account of my week day occupations that you may collect from it how small a portion of time I can save for correspondence &c. A few words in answer to your last letter. I will frankly confess to you that I have lost much if not all of my ambition to become poetically distinguished: & I do not think with Wordsworth that a man may dedicate himself entirely or even in great part to the cultivation of that part of literature, unless he possesses far greater powers of imagination &c than even W. himself, and, (I need not add;) ergo, than I do: or bodily ill-health or mental weak^s prevents him from pursuing to any good purpose studies in useful sciences.

At the same time I think you will not fear that I shall become at any time a bare & barren man of science, such as are so abundant & so appallingly ignorant on this side of Chemistry or Anatomy. Again, even as a dramatist, I cannot help thinking that the study of anat^y phisol-psych: & anthropology applied to and illustrated by history, biography and works of imagination is that w^h is most likely to assist one in producing correct and masterly delineations of the passions: great light w^d be thrown on Shakespeare by the commentaries of a person so educated. The studies then of the dramatist & physician are closely, almost inseparably, allied; the application alone is different; but is it impossible for the same man to combine these two professions in some degree at least?

The science of psychology, & mental varieties has long been used by physicians, in conjunction with the corresponding corporeal knowledge, for the investigation & removal of immaterial causes of disease; it still remains for some one to exhibit the sum of his experience in mental pathology & therapeutics, not in a cold technical dead description, but a living semiotical display a series of anthropological experiments developed for the purpose of ascertaining some important psychical principle—i.e. a tragedy.

Thus far to show you that my studies, pursued as I pledge myself to pursue them, are not hostile, but rather favourable to the developement of a germ w^h I w^d fain believe within me. You will say, "this may be theoretically true, but no such physician has ever yet appeared." I shall have great satisfaction in contradicting you, as Dr. Johnson did the man who denied motion. You talk about too much practice & so forth. I believe that is what is least to be feared; I am very nearly unconnected, am not apt at flattery or the social humiliations to w^h the fashionable physician is bound; am perhaps somewhat independent, & have a competence adequate to my philosophical desires—There are reasons why I should reject too much practice, if it did intrude; really I am much more likely to remain a patientless physician.

And now I will end this unnecessary subject, by telling you that Death's Jestbook goes on like the tortoise slow & sure; I think it will be entertaining, very un-amiable, & utterly unpopular. Very likely it may be finished in the spring or summer; I shall not if I can help it return to England, but shall send it to you or Procter to see what can be done about printing it with the Pygmalion & the other thing whose name I forget, as it will have a certain connection in a leading feature with them: of w^h I believe the former is much the best.

As yet I have hardly any German acquaintance here, as I cannot speak the language very tolerably; from one or two specimens, with w^h I am more intimate & a general external knowledge of the body of students, I can decidedly say of those here at least that they have been causelessly and disgracefully ridiculed in our ignorant & flippant travels & periodicals: There is an appetite for learning, a spirit of

41

diligence, and withal a goodnatured fellow-feeling wholly unparallelled in our old Apoplectic & paralytic Almæ Matres; 9 students out of 10 at this time of the year rise at 5 or 6, study the whole day & night, & Saturday night & sunday morning are set aside for social communication. I never was better employed, never so happy, never so well self-satisfied. I hope to remain here three years at least, I shall then probably visit Berlin, Leipzig, Vienna, some of the Italian curiosities, & finally Paris, for I intend to devote 8 or 10 years to these studies, combined with the languages necessary and a slender thread of practical literature. You see I will not fail of being something by not exercising what talent I have. I feel myself in a measure alone in the world & likely to remain so, for from the experiments I have made I fear I am a non-conductor of friendship, a not-very-likeable person so that I must make sure of my own respect & occupy that part of the brain w^h should be employed in imaginative attachments in the pursuit of immaterial & unchanging good.

I am ashamed of having scribbled a letter so full of myself but I send it because it may entertain you & I think you require some explanation of my way of studying medicine. Shame on you for having anticipated a regular M.D. to arise out of my ashes after reduction in the crucible of German philosophy. Apollo has been barbarously separated by the moderns, I would endeavour to unite him. Of German literature, professors here, Anecdote and news in our next, w^h will not appear before the receipt of your next.

Yours truly
T. L. Beddoes

As P. will certainly not have answered my letter when you are in town at Xmas scold him in your best German. I really will answer him in a German letter if he is so bad again.

Could you find a Prometheus unbound(34) and a Cenci and send them straight and fearlessly to bey *Keil Juden Strasse*?

Keil is my landlord, *bey* is *Chez*.

LETTER XIX

                    To Thomas Forbes Kelsall
                        Götttingen
                        [*Postmark 12 Dec 1925*]

    Lieber Kelsall,—Pardon the evident selfishness of this
second letter, w^h, I hope, will meet you in town; I should be
infinitely obliged to you if you could find time to visit
Devereux Court & obtain from the landlady Mrs. Landers, a
portmanteau w^h I left there, intending to have returned to
England soon. As in all probability this will not happen for
years, (and if it does I shall be very much annoyed,) it will be
better to take these things; to wit, a portmanteau, hat & box,
& writing desk out of the lodgings, where most likely they
would be forgotten, and Mrs. Landers will give them to you
on seeing this letter. If you will then take the trouble to break
open the portmanteau, you will find a miscellany of shirts,
stockings, coats, & manuscripts; the latter I leave entirely, at
your disposal, recommending them, however, to the
dispensation of fire & sword; now take a great stout box of
deal or so & stuff all the shirts & coats & trousers & stockings
in, but none of the books, unless there should happen to be a
Prom: Unbound among them: & if you could, add two or
three copies of the brides' trag:(35) Mr. Rivington will I dare
say allow me a few, for I fear that now they can be little
better than waste paper to him; & add the Prometheus if not
there. Then direct to

Herr Beddoes
Bey Keil Juden Strasse Göttingen
Hannover

and send it off by the Harwich mail, via Hamburg, I shall repeat my thanks upon receiving it: & in return hope to be able to send something that may entertain you at all events bye & bye. At present Anatomy, anatomy, anatomy, of man, dog, & bird occupy so much of my time that you must pardon me for being very dull, my head is full of the origin and insertion of muscles & such names as trachelomastoideces, Cerato-chondroglossus & Bucco pterygo—mylo-genio-cerato: chondro—criccothyreo—syndesmo-pharyngeus. But this beginning is the worst part of the science, which after all is a most important and most interesting one; I am determined never to listen to any meta-physician who is not both anatomist & physiologist of the first rank.

You will not expect much literary intelligence; in Germany as in England the greatest writers of the century are either corporeally or spiritually dead. The theatre is a much duller affair than I imagined, tho' it is much better than the English: of w^h one must altogether despair. Fuimus Troes. But here in the almost innumerable universities you are sure to meet with little galaxies of Hofraths & professors; all men of more or less talent and information. The best here in their several ways are Benecke(36), the English professor, a man who understands more English than most natives; Langenbeck & Hempel, Anatomists, & Surgeons; Krauss, Conradi, and Himly medical professors; Heeren & Saalfeld, historical; & Krause philosophical—besides the Eichhorns & Hugo celebrated Jurists & divines: & the clever old humourous Blumenbach.

One of the most interesting of the idler lectures given here, is by Saalfeld on the history of the French Revolution. This man is a real historian, & no bad orator; but the government people do not much patronize him, as he is extremely free, and if he does not hesitate to condemn Napoleon, has still less remorse in laying bare the infamy of the Polish transaction: he is indeed one of those people, who are dreadful [*torn by seal*] ld continental discipline for his talent [*torn*] moderation; if he had less of the one, he would no longer be [*tole*]rated at the university; if less of the other he would be removed from his catheder by the power of police; & if the latter had effected a total eclipse of the former, he might now be Hofrath & Knight of the Guelphic order.

How does your winter get on? We rise very damp & foggy & the students have been in vain praying for snow that sledging may come in. I wish you a Xmas enriched with the most delightful plum-pudding & pantomime; these are luxuries the names of w^h have scarce yet penetrated this unfashionable region of Germany. There is a shop in the Strand, und zwar at the corner of Bedford Street where you may get shirt-collars at 1s. 3d. a piece, get me eight I beseech thee, & for all things you shall really be paid almost immediately. Once more send me not the portmanteau, hatbox or desk, no boots & no books save as aforesaid. I leave all but coats & trousers, stockings, shirts, neck-cloths, great coat, shirtcollar, drawers & so weit to the mercy and compassion of yourself & him of Southton Row. Visit me with a German commission in return.

Present my compliments to Mrs. Procter; and I will venture to complain to her of the conduct of a certain literary character; I have given up verse, or I w^d write a satire on B. C.(37) & call it Bradypus tridactylos—Leben Sie wohl. Fears not B. C. a second attack from L. E. L.?

I enclose a 1£ payable in London if the Harwich Bank has not broke. I should like to have a few Br. tragedies, but hope they can be procured without paying for them, to me they w^d be dear at ¾.

Addressed to
"T. F. Kelsall Esqre
care of B. W. Procter Esqre
14 Southampton Row
Russell Square
London

45

Letter XX

Postmarks
"Göttingen
7 Mar"
"F.P.O
Mr 13
1826

"Direct
An Herrn Beddoes
bey Eysel
77 Wender Stasse
Göttingen
Hannover"

Today a truant from the old odd bones
And winds of flesh, which, as tamed rocks and stones
Piled cavernously make his body's dwelling,
Have housed man's soul: there, where time's billows
        swelling
Make a deep ghostly and invisible sea
Of melted worlds, antidiluvially
Upon the sand of ever crumbling hours
God-founded, stands the castle, all its towers
With veiny tendrils ivied this bright day
I leave its chambers, and with oars away
Seek some enchanted island where to play.
And what do you, that in the enchantment dwell
And should be raving ever, a wild swell
Of passionate life rolling about the world
Now sunsucked to the clouds, dashed on the curled
Leafhidden daisies; an incarnate storm
Letting the sun through on the meadows yellow;
Or anything except that earthy fellow
That wise dog's brother, man? O shame to tell!
Make tea in Circe's cup, boil the cool well,
The well Pierian, which no bird dare sip

46

But nightingales. There let them kettles dip
Who write their simpering sonnets to it's song
And walk on Sunday's in Parnassus park.
Take thy example from the sunny lark,
Throw off the mantle which conceals the soul,
The many-citied world, and seek thy goal
Straight as a starbeam falls. Creep not nor climb
As they who place their topmost of sublime
On some peak of this planet pitifully,
Dart eaglewise with open wings and fly,
Until you meet the gods. Thus council I
The men who can, but tremble to be great,
Cursed be the fool who taught to hesitate
And to regret: time lost most bitterly.
And thus I write and I dare write to thee,
Fearing that still, as you were wont to do,
You feed and fear some asinine Review.
Let Juggernaut roll on, and we, whose sires
Blooded his wheels and prayed around his fires,
Laugh at the leaden ass in the God's skin.
Example follows precept. I have been
Giving some negro minutes of the night
Freed from the slavery of my ruling spright
Anatomy the grim, to a new story
In whose satiric pathos we will glory.
In it Despair has married wildest Mirth
And to their wedding-banquet all the earth
Is bade to bring its enmities and loves
Triumphs and horrors: you shall see the doves
Billing with quiet joy and all the while
Their nest's the skull of some old King of Nile:
But he who fills the cups and makes the jest
Pipes to the dancers, is the fool o' the feast.
Who's he? I've dug him up and decked him trim
And made a mock, a fool, a slave of him
Who was the planet's tyrant: dotard Death:
Man's hate and dread: not with a stoical breath
To meet him like Augustus standing up,
Nor with grave saws to season the cold cup

Like the philosopher, nor yet to hail
His coming with a verse or jesting tale,
As Adrian did and More: but of his night
His moony ghostliness and silent might
To rob him, to uncypress him i' the light
To unmask all his secrets; make him play
Momus o'er wine by torchlight; is the way
To conquer him and kill; and from the day
Spurned, hissed and hooted send him back again
An unmasked braggart to his bankrupt den.
For death is more "a jest" than life: you see
Contempt grows quick from familiarity.
I owe this wisdom to Anatomy—
Your muse is younger in her soul than mine,—
O feed her still on woman's smiles and wine,
And give the world a tender song once more,
For all the good can love and can adore
What's human, fair and gentle. Few, I know,
Can bear to sit at my board when I show
The wretchedness and folly of man's all
And laugh myself right heartily. Your call
Is higher and more human: I will do
Unsociably my part & still be true
To my own soul: but e'er admire you
And own that you have nature's kindest trust
Her weak and dear to nourish,—that I must
Then fare, as you deserve it, well, and live
In the calm feelings you to others give.

There, Mr. B. C. is your small doggrell ? a punishment, tolerably severe, for your delay in answering my letter; pray be as lazy again and you shall have a "double only" of German hexameters in the Klopstock style.

L. E. L. is at Gottingen too to the confusion of German Ink & paper. Look to 't my Parnassian. I am quite delighted at Mrs. Shelley's overwhelming your charming friend of the New Monthly: he has troubled the manes of Sternhold, Hopkins & Robert Wisdom. Apollo forgive him and make him Laureate for it. Now you must tell me all about the last Last Man.

Have you seen Martin's(38) Deluge; do you like it? And do you know that it is a rascally plagiarism upon Danby? D. was to have painted a picture for the King: subject the opening of yᵉ sixth seal in yᵉ revelations: price 800 guineas: he had collected his ideas and scene, and very imprudently mentioned them publicly to his friends & foes—it appears; Like Campbell and Lord B: and lo! his own ideas stare at him out of Martin's canvass in the institution—this is Last man again—and why does not he paint a last Man?

What do they at the wretched Theatres? any fool: tragedies? Don't talk to me of Magazines; they are vermin I detest; and is Darley(39) delivered yet. I hope he's not a mountain. Write or expect—T. L. B.

Now once more O ye dry
Bones, & once more ye muscles—&c.

I have given up Schiller he's never original. Goethe is something like, though not very: if you can by any means get Taylor's translation of the Iphigenia, read it—Don't believe Lord Gower's Faust, it's full of absurd and ignorant blunders, besides it's evident tameness and lameness.

But what an idle generation you are: why don't you learn German? We Germans learn English I assure you: and write it a little. I would not have doggrelized you if I had had anything to say worth a rotten apple; but I only know about Anatomy now: & Germany partakes of the existing mental stagnation of Europe—We'll try and stir it bye & bye.

Addressed to
    "B. W. Procter Esqʳᵉ
        14 Southampton Row
            Russel Square
                London
                    England

To Thomas Forbes Kelsall
April 1. A bad omen!
[*1826*]

My dear Kelsall,—If you had received all the letters which I had wished to write to you, you would have little to complain on the score of slack correspondency, but really we people in Germany have as little to say as we people in England and my thoughts all run on points very uninteresting to you—i.e. on entrails and blood-vessels; except a few which every now and then assumed an Iambic form towards the never-ending Jestbook; it lies like a snow ball and I give it a kick every now & then out of mere scorn and ill-humour, the 4ᵗʰ act & I may say the 5ᵗʰ are more than half done, so that at last it will be a perfect mouse: but such doggeril—ask Procter else whom I lately visited with a rhyming punishment for his correspondential sin. Ask him too what he's doing? I see nothing about editions of poets &c yet? And I assure you I see a great deal about literature and it's royal society—to wit the Lit. Gaz. which comes regular & dull to the tutor of the Rothschild's who live opposite: what a poetical Famine: you must be reduced to Bernard Barton(40) & Hunt's Blacking Bottles, they are the only classical publications of the season.

However if my friend Death lives long enough to finish his jest book it will come with it's strangenesses, it contains nothing else, like an electric shock among the small critics, & I hope to have the pleasure here of reading a cunning abuse of it from the pen of Jerdan.(41) I'll tell you what, if Procter does not write any more we will not any longer believe that he's Barry C. The spirit of some old picture dealer has got into him; did you see the *signs* that he picked up & took for Correggios; I remember smoking a pipe under them in Shropeshire; do not you? If he scrapes a little he'll find the Marquis of Granby underneath.

On the 26ᵗʰ Febʸ we had the Burschen in all their glory: Blumenbach & Eichhorn—that is to say the stream of flowers & the Squirrel—celebrated the 50ᵗʰ anniversary of their professorships. As soon as it was dark between 5 & 600 of us, horse & foot, assembled each with a torch & formed a two & two procession thro' the town to the house where they were feasting, drew round the square, and on Blumenbachs appearance at the window a short speech was made by the leader followed by several tremendous "vivats!"

He made his speech; we departed and threw our torches into a bonfire. This however was only the halo, the pale outskirt, now comes the thick dazzling centre of the promised Burschen glory—and that was the *commerz*, i.e. a general assemblage of all the different Landsmannschaften here to drink and of course smoke together. I went with the Russians; for we few English don't agree well enough to form a separate club & altogether decline to risk the character of the country by pushing forward as its representatives in this holy alliance. The great ceremony consisted in a long anthem during which half a dozen men with swords took the cap of every one present in rotation off his head and singing the solemn words thrust it on the sword—when the weapons were sheathed to the hilt in their crowns, they were again returned as solemnly to the possessor in state of perforation and replaced on his head as he chaunted an oath "bald ein wahren Bursch zu seyn."

In the end we came to a general attack upon tables benches windows & heads and about 3 o'clock in the morning the flower of the german youth was as drunk as a fidler: intending to hear a lecture at 8. Blumenbach is one of the cleverest men in Germany; his works are distinguished for nicety, acuteness and the minutest acquaintance with the in: and outside of Nature: but in his lecture-room he would be a capital subject for Mathews: he lectures on Natural History, that is his auditors bring his very capital manual in their hands & sit out: in an instant one hears a noise as of Punch on the stairs & the old powdered professor pushes in grunting amid as much laughter as Liston. He then begins a lecture composed of jokes, good stories, imitations, inarticulate sounds & oaths & this being ended goes as he came—a good clever merry old man.

Then there is Langenbeck(42) the Anatomist who was once a barber, he's the Kemble of this Munden: during his lecture he throws himself into a thousand attitudes—starts, points and declaims and paces loftily up and down his little stage—he too is a man of firstrate merit as anatomist and surgeon.

Heeren(43) squeaks like Velluti; Hugo(44) is lame and Bouterwek(45) deaf; this is the story about them—quite a provençal tale.

When young in their travels Heeren fell in love with the wife of a very fierce grenadier; and one evening when the husband was out, went to enjoy a tete a tete with the lady—to prevent interruption he placed his friends as centinels, Bouterwek at the bottom, Hugo at the top of the stairs: the man comes in drunk, gives Bouterwek a box on the ear that knocks him over and deafens him for life, runs up, kicks Hugo all the way down stairs & breaks his leg: breaks into the room and does to Heeren what Bowdler does to Shakspeare. Had the friend of Dr. Johnson who wrote a tragedy the catastrophe of which was castration heard this story he might have produced a noble Gaeteo.

You'd be quite delighted to see how I disguise myself here: no human being w^d imagine that I was anything but the most stoical, prosaic, dull anatomist: I almost outwork the laborious Lauerkrauss—and to tell you truly I begin to prefer Anatomy &c to poetry, I mean to my own, & practically besides I never c^d have been the real thing as a writer: there *shall* be no more accurate physiologist & dissector. Now you must tell me all about the Last Man; I am very glad that Mrs. S[*helley*] has taken it from the New Monthly Fellow—and am sure that in almost every respect she will do much better than either of us: indeed she has no business to be a woman by her books. Remember I wrote twice & don't remember that N° 2 was a rankly selfish effusion.

How I envy you the pleasure of dissecting & laughing at such a grotesque fish as the Improvisatore.(46) Don't be malicious & give it to the reviewers, else I will publish "The

Southampton Bowwindow a Satire on Kelsall." You may look out for some entertainment in "Bristol Macaronics"—it is written by Eagles(47) a very clever fellow, author of a translation of the Batrachomyomachia published by Elton in Lond. Mag.

Benecke who taught Coleridge German here, says that he has a very superficial knowledge of it. From what I know of Kant, i.e. his Anthropology—a very sensible acute man-of-the-world book—I suspect C. has never read him, at all events he has given the English a totally absurd opinion of him. Thank you for the box, because it never came. Do what you will or can with the other things: you are very welcome to Schiller to enrich your upper shelves: I shall not read him ever again. Ask me about poets? &c talk of Anatomists & I'll tell you something. I have left off reading Parnassian foolery? I can bear a satire still tho' and write one as Jest book shall show. Tell me about the last Man. I am very much obliged to Mrs. S. she has saved me the trouble of spreading the secret of Campbell's ears: direct now.

An Herrn &c
bey Straus. 484. Buch Strasse

& give this direction to the late Barry Cornwall, I send his dead body, w^h has the impudence to pretend to live still & does not write even to me,—a wrong man

This is the true S. Pure.—

Does Procter write in Kellsall's Magazine? At the end of my next book shall be Arion (A: wry: one)—a monody on the Death of B. C. with proposals for an edition of his works in usum Delphini—Did I ever pun before? It is anatomy that works in me so wittily. Adieu. T. L. B.

Thank you for the box to day—because it has come. You're right the Cenci is best, because truest. Your inventory was most capital, a legal exercise I presume, particularly the logical division of Woollen stuffs—I for the throat II for the neck III for the wrist. If I had room I could find in my heart to be as tedious as the two kings of Brentford all over again. Why did you send me the Cenci? I open my own page, & see at once what damned trash it all is. No truth or feeling. How the deuce do you, a third & disinterested person, manage to tolerate it? I thank heaven that I am sitting down pretty steadily to medical studies. Labour then can do almost all. Only think of growing old under the laurels of the literary Gazette or Campbell's Mag. Have you seen the Monthly Mag. since its resurrection? Tomorrow I electrify Benecke, who has a considerable indifference to Ld Byron, with Shelley. It will give him a new idea of Englishmen. I sh^d like to see your agony on this Cross—it being Easter week. You dont study Anatomy, Botany, Physiology? Chemistry &c. Come write me.

How many pipes do you smoke every day? I'm quite a novice only three, I will bring Procter a magnificent Meerschaum Kopf if he'll promise to smoke it yellow or you either. Depend on it tis the great help to Metaphysics? Have you seen Leigh Hunt(48) since his return? & what is Elia(49) about? And Darley?

Addressed to
"T. F. Kelsall Esqre
3 Houndwell Lane
Southampton
England"

To Thomas Forbes Kelsall
Göttingen
[*Postmark Oct: 5 1826*]

Lieber Kelsall,—Der, den du so eifrig die schönen Wissenschaften und Lituratur treibst, der in "des Lebens goldenenBaum," den sängenden Baum von den Tausend und einen Nächten suchest, der dem Anbeter der saligen Gottheiten den Musen u. s. w. war unterhaltender kann der Liebhaber von Knaben der flussiger Botaniker und Physiolog mittheilen? u. s. w.

Well I hope that has frightened you however as I can still write a little English & it will be a profitable exercise I will continue in that be-L-E-Led and be-Milmaned tongue. That I have not sent you a letter sooner, will be scarce a cause of complaint or discontent when you learn that, all my sublunary excursions this summer have been botanical ones, & my transluscary (it is a good word & I only recollect it in Drayton's Epistle to Reynolds—has Johnson it) a thought or two for a didactic *B*oem (is that richtig?) on Myology, w^h I was prevented from executing by finding that a preceding genius of the scalpel had led the Muses a dance to his marrowbones and cleaver.

I wish you would come & see me: not only because it would save me the chagrin of dosing you (the shop!) with superfluous solutions of nonsense in ink: but that you might look over my unhappy devil of a tragedy, which is done and done for: it's limbs being as scattered and unconnected as those of the old gentleman whom Medea minced & boiled young. I have tried 20 times at least to copy it fair, but have given it up with disgust, & there is no one here for whose judgement in such things I would give a fig or a teacup without a handle (I have one at the critic's service)

55

consequently neither their praise or blame can lure or sting me onwards—however we must disappoint disappointments by taking them coolly, and throw a chain-bridge across impossibilities or dig a passage under them, or Rubiconize them if one has the good saddle horse Pegasus to ride—& I will find out some way of bestowing my dulness on you in it's ore of illegibility—

I gave you (or did I not ?) a caricature of 3 professors last letter, and now you shall have a little more Goettingen scandal. Tobias Mayer(50) is professor of nat. philosophy, a little fellow in top-boots, with a toothless earthquake of a mouth, & a frosty greycoat—he never can find words—repeats his *alsos* &c & by endeavouring to make up for want of eloquence by violent action, he literally swims through his subject. His dad was a good astronomer & published a famous map of the moon. This "Wife for a month" of the earth revenged the publication of her secret hiding-places on the most natural object of female heavenly malice, his wife thus ingeniously—Top-booted Toby in his lecture was talking of her sonnetship; & came to the subject of her portrait —"among others" said he "Tobias—To-bi-as Mayer—who was —a-mong others was my father."

Tieck has published in the Urania Taschenbuch for 1826 a story called Dichterleben which is a very well worked adventure of Marloe & Green's with Shakspeare. the latter however is too german—& he announces an English translation, probably by himself, to be published at Leipsig under the title of the Lives of Poets: but you are a bad Marlowite or none at all—I like the man on many scores. Here is a Dr. Raupach(51) who lays a tragedy or two in the year—mostly windeggs—but he's the wit of the folks about Melpomene's sepulcre in Germany. Schiller you know took her out of the critical pickle she lies in & made a few lucky galvanic experiments with her, so that the people thought she was alive when she was only kicking. Do you know that a French Dr. of Medicine too, has published a gossiping tour in England in letters, in which he criticises our late friend Barry C. under the name of Procter. The fellow's book is all out of Blackwood excepting a plate or two of autographs out of the

Forgotten Forget me not—Goethe is preparing a new edition of his rhymed & prosy commissions XXXX. vols for 10 dollars who'll buy who'll buy? They are as cheap as oysters if not so swallowable.

In the neighbourhood of Göttingen is a slightly Chalybeate spring & a little inn with a tea garden whither students & Philistines (i.e. townsmen who are not students) resort on Sundays to dance & ride on the Merry-go-round, an instrument of pleasure which is always to be found on such places, and is much ridden by the German students, perhaps because it as well as waltzing produces mechanically the same effects as the week-day hobby-horse the philosophy of Schelling &c doth physically i.e. a giddiness & confusion of the brain.

Behind this Terpsichorean τέμενος rises a woody rocky eminence on which stands a fair high tower & some old mossy and ivyhugged walls, the remains of an old castle called the Plesse: the date of the tower is said to be 963: if this be true it may have earned a citizenship among the semi-eternal stony populace of the planet: at all events it will be older than some hills which pretend to be natural & carry trees and houses—e.g. Monte Nuovo.

On this hill & in the holes and vaults of the old building resides a celebrated reptile, which we have not in England—the salamander. He is to a lizard what a toad is to a frog, slow, fat & wrinkled—of a mottled black & yellow, it is true that under his skin one finds a thick layer of a viscid milky fluid of a peculiar not disagreeable smell which the beast has the power of ejecting when irritated & by this means might for a short time resist the power of fire.

Where the vulgar fable has its origin I am altogether ignorant, I believe it comes from the middle ages; from the monkish writers of natural history perhaps—& they might have had a spite against the poor amphibium, because he is unorthodox enough to live a long while after you have removed his stomach & intestines—& therefore condemned him to the flames for impiety against the belly gods Ἀδηφαγία & Ἀκρατοπότης. The servants at the altars of these thundering deities (v. Euripides Cyclops 327) may adduce

57

physiological authority for the immateriality of their adored Paunch. J. Baptista van Helmont placed the soul, which he nicknamed Archæus, in the stomach & whatever the clergy knew more about the spirit in question I do not think they are inclined to let the cat out of the bag. This is a pleasant doctrine for aldermen and Kings, the dimensions of the soul perhaps corresponding with the size of its habitation: only they must beware of purges it would be a mishap to leave ones soul in a close-stoolpan like George the 2nd.

To return to our Maria-spring, the aforesaid tenement or tenements of fantastictoeness: & what I had intended to tell you: it was here that an unhappy Hungarian who came to Göttingen three or 4 years ago to study medicine, & had wandered to propitiate his Archüus with beer & tobacco at this place was smitten with the charms of the tavern-keepers daughter: she was insensible & he desperate: he left Göttingen & built a hut under a rock in the Plesse wood where he lived 2 years, descending occasionally to feed his eyes upon the beauties of the cruel one. But either the lady departed or his passion burnt out, for at the end of this time the hermitage was left by its love-lorn founder & it now remains as an object of curiosity for folks, who see it: hear his tale & laugh at it.

Such is alas! the state of sentiment in this part of Germany: & probably if Werter's hermitage stood here it would be equally profaned—hard-heartedness & worldly prudence has it's paw upon the poor planet: and as Chaucer sung long ago Pity is dead and buried in gentle heart—but we have lost the sepulchre—And we fellows who cannot weep without the grace of onions or hartshorn, who take terror by the nose, light our matches with lightning, have plucked the "tempest winged chariots of the deep"—of its winds & imped its pinions with steam. We who have little belief in heaven and still less faith in man's heart, are we fit ministers for the temple of Melpomene? O age of crockery! no—let Scandal & Satire be the only reptiles of the soul-abandoned corse of literature—About Anne Boleyn. G. D. Joanna &c

58

I

Come with me thou gentle maid,
The stars are strong and make a shade
Of yew across your mother's tomb
Leave your chamber's vineleaved gloom
Leave your harpstrings, loved one,
"Tis our hour." the robber said.
Yonder comes the goblin's sun
For when men are still in bed
Day begins with the old dead.
Leave your flowers so dewed with weeping
And our fevrish baby sleeping,
Come to me, thou gentle maid
"Tis our hour," the robber said.

II

To the wood whose shade is night
Went they in the owls moonlight,
As they passed the common wild
Like a murderous jester smiled
Dimpled twice with Nettly graves.
You may mark her garment white
In the night wind how it waves:
The night wind to the churchyard flew
And whispered underneath the yew,
"Mother Churchyard, in my breath,
I've a lady's sigh of death."
"Sleep thou there, thou robber's wife,"
Said he clasping his wet knife.

Dr. Raupach

Direct (if you answer before March) Bey Ramsahl. Post Strasse—I have not been out [*of*] Göttingen now for a year— i.e. any distance, & shall probably not leave it for as long a space. What is der seeliger 𝒦*ornwall* about? Adieu, adieu, adieu.

Have you written no prologue this year for the Th. *royal* Southton or have you dropped that since the retirement of Mrs. Hamblin? T. L. B.

Addressed to
   T. F. Kelsall Esqre
     at Admiral Bligh's C.B.
      Fareham
      Hants

LETTER XXIII

To Bryan Waller Procter
October 9th 1826

My dear Procter,—This Göttingen life is little productive of epistolary materials or of any adventure interesting beyond the town walls; and I have not been six miles from the circuit of these during the last year. However, I meditate and must perform a pilgrimage to Dresden, for the sake of its pictures, and then I hope to pick out a few plums to communicate to you.

These matters, I take it for granted, retain their interest for you, because I have a lingering attachment to them, and in sincerity I acknowledge that you possess a truer and more steady feeling for the beautiful in imagination; and the law studies will probably only compress and concentrate it. You will give me leave to believe that you will not and cannot entirely abandon the studies and labours which have many years pretty exclusively possessed you, and by which you have obtained a distinguished reputation; and if you do not, I shall take it. Me you may safely regard as one banished from a service to which he was not adapted, but who has still a lingering affection for the land of dreams; as yet, at least, not far enough in the journey of science to have lost sight of the old two-topped hill.

I wish, indeed, that the times were more favourable to the cultivators of dramatic literature, which from a thousand causes appears to be more and more degraded from its original dignity and value among the fine arts. And yet I believe that the destined man would break through all difficulties and re-establish what ought to be the most distinguished department of our poetic literature; but perhaps enough has already been done, and we ought to be content with what times past have laid up for us. If literature has fallen into bad hands in England, it is little worse off than in Germany, for living and active are few writers above a secondary rank, and they almost unknown beyond the shadow of the double eagle's wings.

Jean Paul(52) is lately dead, and a new edition of his voluminous writings is proceeding from the press.

I have read little of his, and that little has pleased me less. In his happier moods he resembles Elia, but in general he is little better than a pedantical punster.

Tieck has made a good little story by threading together the few facts we have of Marlowe's life, and an English translation is advertised by a Leipzig bookseller, probably by himself. When it appears I shall send it to you by the first opportunity, without waiting for your order.

A quantity of our modern indifferent fellows have been cheaply reprinted by different speculating booksellers. It is a pity they have no good selector, who could spare them the pains of recondemning paper and print to the re-awaking of such trash. It would be as reasonable of dyers to reprint the London waistcoats and breeches of 1810 or '16; for a pattern or a poem of this sort are equally long-lived, and deserve to be so.

In the neighbourhood is a little lake, See-Burger-See. We went there botanising a few weeks ago, and were entertained by our boatman with a genuine legend. A castle had formerly stood on the edge of the water, and the ruins of it still exist on the rocks and under the waves. It was formerly inhabited by a knight who had a confidential cock and a prying servant. Once a month the master, to keep his ears awake to the language of his crowing oracle, partook of a mysterious dish; and it was decreed that whenever a second pair of ears were able to receive and comprehend Chanticleer's conversation, the castle should fall. At last, then, the servant removed the cover of the monthly viand and found a snake under it: he tasted some of this broiled worm of the tree of knowledge, and was from that day forth an eavesdropper of the confidential twitters in sparrows' nests and hen-coops. The prophetic cock soon began to use fowl language, and proclaim the approaching downfall of the towers of burg. The servant who had translated colloquies between fly and fly, bee and flower, did not fail to comprehend the warning; rushed to his master, who was already on his horse and riding out of the castle gate: the walls tumbled, the tower bowed, the groom rushed after his master and seized the horse's tail; the knight plunged his spurs into the sides of his steed, leapt to land, and left his treacherous servant among the waves and ruins.

Here are also the Gleichen, two castles belonging to the family of Ernst von Gleichen, famous for having two wives: W. Scott has told the story somewhere. A grave is shown at Erfurt as containing the relics of the three, and at one of his castles a large bed; but it appears that this three-headed matrimony is fictitious and altogether unsupported by historical documents. These castles overlook a prettyish village, which was a favourite haunt of poor Burger the ballad-writer. He was a private teacher in Göttingen, and probably starved or at all events hastened through the gates of death by poverty and care. Schiller was supposed to be envious of him, and did him a great deal of mischief by ill-natured criticism; but Bürger had more notion of the right translunary thing than his reviewer. About Weber? What grief at the death? His fellow-countrymen and fellow fiddlers were well-pleased with his burial or intended burial honours.

I wish you joy of Sir R. ——G 's(53) being out of the way; you may sit upon a woolsack yet. Was it to fill your sheet that you sent a good deal of advice or remonstrance in your last to me? Perhaps you forget it. I only mention it to observe that it is a little singular that a dramatic writer, a person who has observed and knows something of human character, should take the trouble to attempt corrections of the incorrigible, and pour so much oil upon a fire by way of extinguishing it. Allow me to say that you are mistaken if you think I willfully affect any humour; even that of affecting nothing. I always make a point of agreeing with everything that a fool pleases to assert in conversation, and only combat assertions or opinions of a person for whom I have respect. *Verbum sap.* You people in England have a pretty false notion of the German character, and flatter yourselves with your peculiar and invincible insular self-complacency that you know all about it; for national vanity I believe after all you are unequalled. The Frenchmen rests his boast on the military glories of *la grande nation*; the German smokes a contemptuous pipe over the philosophical works of his neighbours; but the Englishman will monopolise all honourable feeling, all gentle breeding, all domestic virtue, and indeed has ever been the best puritan. Is the revolution in the "Quarterly" true? The last number we had here did smack somewhat of "Blackwood." Present my best compliments to Mrs. Procter, and don't let your answer be as dull as this.

Yours
T. L. Beddoes.

Recollect I write from Göttingen.

"Death's Jest Book" is finished in the rough, and I will endeavour to write it out and send it to you before Easter: at

63

all events I think parts of it will somewhat amuse you: ὁι πολλοί will find it quite indigestible. W. A. Schlegel is professor at Bonn, a ten years old Prussian university on the Rhine. His brother Friedrich is in Austria, and writes puffs for the Holy Alliance. No Austrian is allowed to study here— Göttingen is so famous for liberality. I intend to study Arabic and Anglo-Saxon soon. I have just bought three salamanders. They are pretty, fat, yellow and black reptiles, that live here in the ruins of an old castle in the neighbourhood; on the Hartz I hear they are larger. It is not a bad retributory metempsychosis for the soul of a bullying knight.

LETTER XXIV

To Thomas Forbes Kelsall
Postmark
Göttingen
20 April: 1827

My dear Kelsally,—This is an odd bit of paper, but you must excuse it; the company of stationers shut up their doors as soon as the "company of clouds" take their station in Apollo's highroad: or to speak un-euphuistically the paper-vendors are in bed; I have no Gottingen vellum for I seldom write a letter, and feeling a little that way inclined, a rare state of inspiration at present with me, I shall not thwart the rising deity because the rags on w^h he is to vent his fury are not exalted to the highest perfection of Paperhood. Forgive me if I write bad English; I am just now the only English person here, and live in the most enviable solitude, the few Germans I associate at all with are away as it is vacation time, and I am waited upon by a slow Teutonic damsel as speechless as the husband of the Silent Woman(54) could desire.

I would not believe your enemy if he said that you were so indolent as you desire yourself. I know what indolence and idleness is too pretty well, and am not now altogether free from attacks of these evil ones—and recollect with dread the state of mental flatulence w^h : I endured for sometime, really in a great measure because, thanks to the state of education in England, I did not know what to study. You probably describe a passing mood of this nature otherwise— but Conscience is ever the best adviser.

I read very little of the German polite literature as they call it, but lately I was induced to look into some of Tieck's original writings in consequence of the very agreeable impression I received from some critical remarks of his on Shakspeare—(much truer & more imbued with a feeling of the actual existence of Shakspeare's men & women, than the cold philosophizing abstractions of Schlegel) (I can pronounce that name rightly now. Jeer no more at my German!) He (Tieck) as B. C. says in a parenthesis, has written a good deal—Tales—and Dramatic Tales—some of these latter are very long—mostly in 2 parts of 5 acts each but excessive agreeable reading, with a vein of gentle tonic humour w^h never lets one sleep; he is never very strong or deep, but altogether displays more general power as a dramatist than any of the more celebrated Germans. He particularly delights in presenting nursery tales in a dramatic form? he has a Puss in Boots, Blue Beard, Fortunatus and little Red Riding hood. This last is short but a most delightful absurdity. The dramatis persone are the heroine—Grandmother. A Huntsman who is in search of the Wolf. The Wolf (Mr. McCready's part as villain) Dog, & Robin-Redbreasts, special allies of Red Riding hood's because of their sympathy in colour—and a Cuckoo—The scene discovers the Grandmother sitting alone on a Sunday morning and expecting her little relative, she comes with some cake and chatters with the old lady some time is particularly eloquent in praise of her red riding hood—she goes and leaves the housedoor open to the dismay of the Old lady—on

Redridinghood's return thro' the Forest she makes acquaintance with the Redbreasts and meets the Huntsman who announces the incursion of a ravenous wolf.

To this principal personage the reader is now introduced —he relates his history to the dog, how in his youth he was a cosmopolite and philanthrope, deserted his barbarous clanswolves and came into the village to gain knowledge and to be useful in his generation: here he became acquainted with a shewolf of the neighbourhood whose person was peerless and after whose spotless Life and amiable manners one might have written A whole duty of Shewolves: however his vita Nuova like Dante's was broken off by the death of this his fairly fair in that she was murdered by a peasant at her evenings repast on a lamb: & now Sir Isgrim is become Childe Harold in Wolfs clothing, he condemns the canine, hates and vows vengeance on the human kind, and devotes to the manes of his lost lady the head of little R. R. whose father slew the Fornarina and Queen Elizabeth, and Ninon & Mrs. Fry of she-wolfhood: the dog his friend is a good-natured fellow, a temporizing phlegmatic Græculus esuriens, who praises all government as long as he has a bone to pick; attempts to dissuade Sir I., fails & retires.

Little R. R. meantime has got her custard & pot of honey to take to her Grandmother this evening altho' it is growing dark & now follows a scene of omens & warnings—she & another little girl blow off the seeds of dandelions heads to see how long they shall live—the other blows a long while in vain, but the Scarlet woman with one puff sends all her pappers adrift—but vain is this omen of Flora's, R. R's father is probably a radical & takes in the Mechanic's Magazine for his little one is a complete philosopher and retorts the exultation of her fellow-dandelion-blower by reducing the phenomenon to natural principles—she has blown the dandelions head clean at one puff because she has good lungs & will therefore live longest and sends away tother little one crying: a peasant crosses her and advises her not to go this evening thro' the wood as it is nearly dark and the wolf's abroad: this has no effect & now her household gods stir themselves for the last time and produce a wonder to

66

detain her—enter the Cuckoo:—

> Cook—for Grandam-koo another time
> Gook not koo the wood koo-night
> Gook look koo through
> Gook brook koo who
> Gooks lurks koo the there
> Cuck a wolf or a bear
> Cuck cannot cuck any more
> Spooking for kinds is a bore
> Cuckoo—Woe to thee Cuckoo

> Little R.—Cuckoo you fool learn to speak
> better English.
> Koo-night indeed ha! ha!
> (enter Dog.)

> Dog.—Bough-vow. Bough-vow
> (probably a cockney dog)
> Bow your way home
> How couldst thou come
> Bow alone vow—
> Boughs cloudy are.
> Cows browse not there,
> Vows wolf to tear
> Bow thou—thee to bits
> I bow now and quit. (exit.)

She goes on: reaches her granddams Chamber. The wolf
enters lying on a bed and R. R. admires the size of her nose:
eyes: teeth: at this cue the wolf seizes her & in the struggle
the bedcurtains fall before them, the Robins fly in at the
window & discover the murder to the Huntsman who is
without: he shoots into the room and kills the wolf—Curtain
falls.

This is a trifle—but Fortunatus, Emperor Octavius, &
Genevra contain very beautiful things & are more animated
with a dramatic spirit than any of those tasteless fatulity

plays with the translations of w^h Mr. Gillies(55) has so liberally *presented* our Blackwood reading public. I am studying Arabic & think of taking the field against Heber(56) in the winter—I am reading Dante's Vita Nuova—it is a simple Confessio amantis—interwoven with curious Ptolemean Astronomy & Catholic Theology—the sonnets &c are much more to my taste than that Petrarcan eau d'Hippocrene sucré: did P. & Laura ever come into your head in the scene between Slender & Sweet Anne? My next publication will probably be a dissertation on Organic Expansion; or an enquiry into the laws of the Growth & Restoration in organized matter.

I am now already so thoroughly penetrated with the conviction of the absurdity & unsatisfactory nature of human life that I search with avidity for every shadow of a proof or probability of an after-existence both in the material & immaterial nature of man. Those people, perhaps they are few, are greatly to be envied who believe honestly and from conviction in the Xtian doctrines: but really in the New T. it is difficult to scrape together hints for a doctrine of immortality—Man appears to have found out this secret for himself & it is certainly the best part of all religion and philosophy, the only truth worth demonstrating: an anxious Question full of hope & fear, & promise for wh. Nature appears to have appointed one solution—Death. In times of revolution & business, and even now the man who can lay much value in the society, praise, or glory of his fellows may forget, and he who is of a callous phlegmatic constitution may never find the dreadful importance of the doubt. I am haunted for ever by it; & what but an after-life can satisfy the claims of the oppressed in nature, satiate endless & admirable love & humanity & quench the greediness of the spirit for existence: but

> As an almighty night doth pass away
> From an old ruinous city in a desert,
> And all its cloudy wrecks sink into day:
> While every monstrous shape and ghostly wizard,
> That dwelled within the cavernous old place

Grows pale and shrieks and dies in its dismay:
And then the light comes in and flowery grace
Covers the sand, & man doth come again
& Live rejoicing in the new-born plain:
So you have seen great gloomy centuries,
(The shadow of Rome's Death) in w^h did dwell
The men of Europe, shudder & arise,
So you have seen break up that smoke of Hell
Like a great superstitious snake, uncurled
From the pale temples of the awaking world.

These lines were written in the album of a man who had busied himself in his pretty advanced life with political speculations watched the progress of the American and French revolutions with interest and expectation. No English person or English reader in Göttingen c^d or w^d understand them. For this reason I began to think they might be good & have therefore rewritten them for you

T. L. B.

Addressed to
"T. F. Kelsall Esqre
Fareham
Hants

> *To* Thomas Forbes Kelsall
> [*Postmark*]
> *Göttingen*
> *13 May 1827*

'One of my friends sent me a week or two ago the following poem, w^h he had transcribed out of an old album in the library at Hamburg. The date 1604 was on the binding of it—He cannot give a more decided description of the book. The lines are written in a neat old English hand.

> My thoughts are winged with hopes, my
>   hopes with Love,
> Mount love unto the moon in clearest night
> And saie, as she doth in the heaven move
> In earth so wanes and waxeth my delight,
> And whisper this but softly in her ears *
> How oft doubt hange the head and trust shed teares.
> And you, my thoughts that seem mistrust to varye †
> If for mistrust my mistris do you blame
> Saie, though you alter yet you do notvarye
> As shee doth change and yett remaine the same:
> Distrust doth enter hartes but not infect
> And love is sweetest seasoned with suspect.
> If shee, for this, with clouds do mask her eyes
> And make the heavens dark with her disdaine,
> With windie sights ‡ disperse them in the skyes,
> Or with thy teares desolve them in to rayne
> Thoughts, hopes and love returne to me no more
> Till Cinthia shyne as shee hath done before. W. S.

'I have communicated the lines, with a strict regard ever to the interpunctuation, exactly as I received them.' (I too—T.

L. B.) Beneckein the Wunschelrathe —(Divining Rod) A dead Göttingen periodical No. 34. April 27. 1 81 8. Gothegave this translation in his periodical Vol. 2. No. 3 Stuttgard 1820. p. 32

Here grunteth the old pig of Weimar—

*　　*　　*　　*

Göthe has done no good here, first he says out of an album of 1604—whereas the book was bound in 1604—was it bound before or after the sheets were written on—I suppose according to English custom, it was a blank book bought by some dilletante for a scrap: M.S. book—Such are seldom very soon filled—and therefore in all probability the lines were written, here at least, in the latter days of Shakspeare. Two lines of it w^h I need not point out to you give the thing a possibility—But who is Cynthia? In the sonnets &c is no Cynthia mentioned & altogether there is scarce any evidence of Shakspeares being in love in a sonneteering way—he was probably too well acquainted with the tricks of Authorship, too intimate with the artifice and insincerity of poetry to think of availing himself of it in any serious passion at this time of his life (see Sonnet 130).

His sonnets I take to be early** productions dictated by an ardent attachment to W. H. who was younger†† than himself, and written all before he had become a poetical artist. It may be that these lines were written hastily by him for W. H. or perhaps some Court gentlemen to serve as a complimentary poem or song for his lady—But is there any

* Shak. bestowed ears rather on such erratic stars as Bottom than on the Moon
† (to carry, of course T.L.B)
‡ Benecke says this is rightly spelt for the time; taking for granted that the verses were written *before the book was bound*, and swallowing the W.S. It remedies a jingle between sighs and skies—so far good.
** See sonnet 32 & 21
†† S. 96 compared with the exaggerating melancholy 73rd

necessity for raising so great a spirit, is it absolutely necessary that no other W. S. co^d have written these lines? The internal evidence is so little satisfactory to my feelings that I cannot think Goethe pardonable for his temerity in printing Shakspeares name at the end of the verses upon such deficient historical grounds. Compare too the Italian frivolity the careless superficial playfulness, the constrained elegance & roundness of this little bit of verse with the deep & ardent expressions of that wondrous book of sonnets where he has turned his heart inside out & given us all to read all that the tender & true spirit had written on the walls of his chamber,: the former is as the dimple of the coquetting man of the world to the ἀυηρίθμον γελασμα—the starry tremulous universal smile of an ocean of passion, which ebbed & flowed about the roots of a love, as firm & sacred as the foundations of the world.

So far from being ready to attribute anything he c^d have written to S. I am inclined to deny the authenticity of many smaller pieces & songs such as that to Silvia in 2 Gent, of Verona. At this period of his life—(40 years of age) his spirit was at rest, he was wearied of the "light airs & recollected terms. Of those most brisk and giddy-paced times," that feeling was awakened to full consciousness, w^h dictated the true, self condemning expressions of the 110th Sonnet, & he was yearning for the quiet truth of enjoyment, the peace of life. He had long learned that there were mysteries in the feelings and passions of the soul, some of w^h he had too rashly revealed; that the most exquisite happiness is silent, it's delights unutterable. He had uncovered to profaner eyes some of the farthest sanctuaries of the heart, he had lent to vulgar tongues the sacred language of truth & divine passion & it was this repentance & sorrow for the violation, which speaks so sorrowfully in that little poem, which deterred him from printing the compositions in w^h he had made his own soul a thoroughfare for the world. At this time, wearied and disgusted as he clearly was with the fate w^h had necessitated him to feed cold eyes with the emotions of his eternal nature, c^d he have so returned to the cold conceits with w^h he had dallied before he had learned the truth & sacredness of

72

human feeling? I cannot think so.

But that an old fellow of letter-press, an author of our days, who w^d send the paper wet with his own heart's blood to the printer that fools might wonder & bookmen adore his art, sh^d think so, is what we can but expect from this vulgar prostituted age. I fear that Printing is a devil whom we have raised to feed & fatten with our best blood & trembling vitals. I (excuse, if you laugh at, this egotism of insignificance) will not again draw the veil from my own feelings to gratify the cold prying curiosity of such, as the million are, & will remain T. L. B—

You will hardly thank me for this letter, I have gone on with it without attending to the laws & purposes of correspondence—but send it that you may gather from the expressions a way of thinking w^h grows upon me daily—Do you think I am right both with relation to the lines w^h have occasioned them & the sentiment in general or in neither? I hope your instinct will lead you thro' this labyrinth of remark, note Query—it looks like a skreen full of puzzles—

Addressed to
T. F. Kelsall Esq
Fareham
Hants

To Thomas Forbes Kelsall
A Tuesday in Oct. Göttingen
[*Postmark*] *21 Oct. 1827*

My dear Kelsall,—This week has been more productive
of epistolary fruits to me, than the foregoing 3 months. On
Saturday came a young Scotch Lawyer, Mr Fraser, with a
note from the conveyancing phœnix which has arisen from
the ashes of the late B. C. gent, and a tall Swiss who expects
to become professor of the Teutonic language in Univ.
Londin—the latter acquaintance pleased me much the more
of the two, he is a man of good, & extensive Education with
an interest for all human sciences and arts—and smoked his
new bought large Göttingen pipewell. The Law gentleman is
Editor of the new foreign Review who was recruiting for
contributors & wanted to catch me: however I am not
magazinish inclined and do not augur well of the
undertakings of young Editors, who are well informed of
hardly anything but their own superior capacities—an occult
science enough; still as it is always as well to give Cerberus a
sop, when one has a thought of one day retreading the
Tartarus emeticus of Modern literature, I treated him to a
promise of an article upon modern Hebrew literature of the
unholy kind.

The writer of this is to be a native of Odessa, a man who
has a quantity of brain but no breeches, and for Hebrew
utterly incomparable, for I presume there are few Jews or
Christians pious folks who can or have translated Schiller,
written songs &c in that desolated and abandoned language.
Moreover he utterly refused to button up his reason & belief
in the prophetical old clothes into which the shoulders of the
events of later years have been thrust—he hath alas never
been christened, is a deep philosopher, a lauder of Spinosa:
in fact a choice morsel for the torch which Calvin &c.

brandished: a fellow after Julians heart: but then he would sup with the devil must needs have a long spoon, to toss some of his broth into the trough at which David's sow doth squeal and wag her curly tale—and that is wanting to my Russian Pyrrho. This treatise, if I can get him to write it, will be admirable for all people who know or don't know anything of the Jews—

The Mr Fraser brought too a copy of his Bijou for w^h Procter has written. This for Göttingen is an unfortunate name. Blumenbach tells in his "At home" on Natural history a tale of M. Bigou in Paris, who was a collector too of a peculiar and odious description, a Nightman Errant who went batfowling after Excrement of every species of every genius. This man may have been inspired by the God of the Kamtschatkadaler, Jupiter Rutka, who fell in love, according to their sacred traditions, with his own ordure when it was frozen, and believed it to have been a fair maiden, such as they are in Kamschatka, till his intreaties had melted her icy bosom, & his nose was convinced of the error of his heart.

You wish to convince me of my error regarding the publication of expressions of feeling: which are ours for the enjoyment of domestic happiness: I repeat that I regard it as a profanation: does not Shakespeare grant it, & who but him had built an ear for the tyrant vulgar where it might eaves drop & overhear the secret communings of human souls?—

It would be worth while to consider the domestic lives of all the greater poets of modern times; for the ancients lacked those refinements and domestic enjoyments of which we speak. Shakspeare, Dante, Milton, all who have come next to the human heart, had found no object in life to satiate the restless yearnings of their hearts & appease at the same time the fastidious cravings of their imaginations. Dissatisfaction is the lot of the poet if it be that of any being, & therefore the gushings of the spirit; their pourings out of their innermost on imaginary topics because there was no altar in their home worthy of the libation. It is good that we should see from these involuntary overflows of the soul what it is that moves within us: such is the manna of the tree of life. But to force it, to count one's fingers and take the sweat of our Grub street brows for the true juice, the critical drops w^h the souls struggles must press from our veins ere it be genuine: to pant for fame, to print & correct our tame frigid follies, to be advertised in the newspapers with the praise of the Lit. Gaz. is really abundantly pitiful and as ridiculous as the crowning of the pedant Petrarch. To annoy and puzzle the fools and amuse oneself with their critical blunders is the only admissible plea for printing for any one who has been a few years from school—excepting poverty, Mr. Croly: excepting avarice, Sir Walter(57).

Göthe has, as you probably by this time know, published an interlude to Faust, in which he gives him as a play fellow our fair witch of Troy, Helena, who bestows her name on the piece—I have read it once and not very carefully through and found nothing very extraordinary: fine passages which remind one of Euripides and Iphigenie, & graces such as his better productions contain are there: & a spirit plays upon the surface of his fancies which announces the presence of a creator, but on the whole it is not palpable, it dances o'er the brain and leaves no footstep there. Still there is something irritating in it & it is probably a hieroglyphic in which the man pourtrays the passage of antique fable into the middle ages: the best thing perhaps is a great fearful old housekeeper of Menelaus who frightens Helen from Sparta to the castle where Faustus receives her, follows & threatens her, and at the end of the piece lays aside the mask, mantle and cothurn & discovers herself to be Mephistophiles. A review of it is to be inserted in the foreign review from the pen of the professor of Northern Literature elect in London.

I can really send you nothing of my own, I have a pretty good deal in fragments which I want to cement together and make a play of—among them is the last Man. They will go all into the Jest book—or the Fool's Tragedy—the historical nucleus of which is an isolated and rather disputed fact, that Duke Boleslaus of Münsterberg in Silesia was killed by his court fool a.d. 1377. but that is the least important part of the whole fable I have dead game in great quantities but when or how it will be finished Æsculapius alone knows: I will give you a song out of it w^h seems to me bad—but my English vocabulary is growing daily more meagre, and I have neither much time nor much inclination to keep up my poetical style by perusing our writers: I am becoming daily more obtuse for such impressions and rather read a new book on anatomy than a new poem English or German.

Yet let me assure you that your idea of my merits as a writer is extravagantly surpassing my real worth: I w^d really not give a shilling for anything I have written, nor sixpence for anything I am likely to write. I am essentially unpoetical in character, habits & ways of thinking: and nothing but the desperate hunger for distinction so common to young gentlemen at the Univ^y, ever set me upon rhyming. If I had possessed the conviction that I could by any means become an important or great dramatic writer I would have never swerved from the path to reputation: but seeing that others who had devoted their lives to literature, such as Coleridge and Wordsworth, men beyond a question of far higher originality and incomparably superior poetical feeling and Genius, had done so little, you must give me leave to persevere in my preference of Apollo's pill box to his lyre, & should congratulate me on having chosen Göttingen instead of Grub street for my abode—

Indeed all young verse grinders ought to be as candid and give way to the really inspired. What would have been my confusion & dismay, if I had set up as a poet, and later in my career anything real and great had start up amongst us & like a real devil in a play frightened into despair & futerity the miserable masked wretches who mocked his majesty.

These are my real and good reasons for having at last rendered myself up to the study of a reputable profession in which the desire of being useful may at least excuse me altho I may be unequal to the attempt to become a master in it; & I assure you that the approbation which you have pleased to bestow upon a very sad boyish affair, that same Brides Tr: which I w^d not even be condemned to read through for any consideration, appears to me a remarkable & in-comprehensible solecism of your otherwise sound literary judgement.

Now it being a star and moonlight night and a bevy of

ladies crossing the water in a boat well let them sing—but methinks its damned moorish & obscure

Wild with passion, sorrow-beladen,
Bend the thought of thy stormy soul
On it's home,on it's heaven, the lovedmaiden
And peace shall come at her eyes' control
Even so night's starry rest possesses
With its gentle spirit these tamed waters
And bids the wave with weedy tresses
Embower the ocean's pavement stilly
Where the sea girls lie, the mermaid daughters
Whose eyes not born to weep
More palely lidded sleep
Than in our fields the lily
And sighing in their rest
More sweet than is it's breath
And quiet as it's death
Upon a lady's breast.

Heart high beating, triumph bewreathed
Search the record of loves gone by
And borrow the blessings by them bequeathed
To deal from out of thy victory's sky.
Even so throughout the midnight deep
The silent moon doth seek the bosoms
Of those dear mermaid girls asleep
To feed its dying rays anew
Like to the bee on earthly blossoms
Upon their silvery whiteness
And as the rainbow brightness
Of their eyelash's dew,
And kisseth their limbs o'er;
Her lips where they do quaff
Strike starry tremors off
As from the waves our oar.

You hardly deserve it for the last time you did not say thankye for a great something snake wh. I had caught and caged in a sonnet for you, however so much to show you what you might have expected and to induce you to thank the disposition of providence w^h will preserve to you any part of your personal property which you w^d wantonly devote for a box of such like. Such verses as these & their brethren will never be preserved to be pasted on the inside of the coffin of our planet. Thank you for Mr. Hood, he seems to be pretty tolerable: & not at all in danger to be too deep for his readers. Apollo have mercy on him.

Yours truly
T. L. B.

If you are rich & charitably inclined or are acquainted with such, you can send to Coutts on my account any small contributions for my un-Xtian Russian: he wants to take his M.D. but it costs alas £30—I dunn all my acquaintance. Tell me how many pence you give us.

Addressed to
    T. F. Kelsall Esqre
        Fareham
          Hants
            England

LETTER XXVII

My dear Kelsall,—On the 17th I hope to be in London, and on the following Saturday to leave it; as imperious necessity requires my presence at Göttingen on ye 30th & something still more imperious than necessity calls me to another Continental town in the Netherlands where I must consume a day or two on my passage. In fact as soon as I am M.A. my first desire will be to step into the Ostend packet, w^h I sh^d do directly after leaving Oxford, if I had not some Law business wh will keep me about 2 days in London. Nothing can equal my impatience & weariness of this dull idle pampered isle.

Letters & invitations without number w^h have been or must be answered by return of post in the same way prevent me from being more diffuse. I sh^d be very glad to see you if possible, but do not be in a hurry to be disappointed. You will easily even in the country stumble upon a person as indifferent to fine situation or nearly so as

Yours truly
T. L. B.

My landlady is
Mrs. Landers
6 Devereux Court
Temple Bar
London.

Addressed to
T. F. Kelsall Esqre
Fareham
Hants

> *To* Thomas Forbes Kelsall
> postmark
> [*Gottingen*] *27 Feby 1829*

My dear Kelsall,—A day sooner or later than this letter, will arrive, I hope, at No. 3 Fig tree court at length, the celebrated Fool's Tragedy or D's J book. I have written to Procter announcing the fact to him and leaving to him whether he will interest himself about its furtherance to the press, as I acknowledge I have no right to expect it from him. If you are in town get it either from him or Bourne(58) & be critical. There is some wretched comic part in it, w^h I cannot improve nor give up—I hope however that it is no unworthy contemporary of the Briton Chief. Have you read anything of the new Mr. Montgomery?(59) He appears actually a good deal worse than the old. Allan C's anniversary(60) I have seen here, & I suppose shall never see another: All the folks seem to have been trying who could be most stupid. Procter's Temptation however is a redeeming exception & makes the book worth something till he reprints it. There is a freedom, and a degree of poetical and dramatic management in it w^h I only regret to see in such company, & thrown away on a purposeless scene for a temporary purpose. I should like to see a play in that way & why could not & should not he give it us? He is only about as much too brief as I am too long-winded; but he can correct his failing more easily.

My cursed fellows in the jestbook would palaver immeasurably & I could not prevent them. Another time it shall be better, that is to say if the people make it worth my while to write again. For if this affair excites no notice I think I may conclude that I am no writer for the time & generation, and we all know that posterity will have their own people to talk about. You are, I think disinclined to the stage: now I confess that I think this is the highest aim of the dramatist, & and should be very desirous to get on it. To look down on it is a piece of impertinence as long as one chooses to write in the form of a play, and is generally the result of a consciousness of one's own inability to produce anything striking & affecting in that way. Shakespeare wrote only for it, Ld B. despised it, or rather affected this as well as every other passion, which is the secret of his style in poetry & life.

In my preface I have made use of an essay on Tragedy by Southey's Dutch friend Bilderdijk(61) which is, I think, extremely satisfactory and establishes the independence of the English Drama of all Greek authority on an undeniable historical foundation. B. to be sure is directly opposed to the English in taste, but this is nothing to the purpose, he has given us good weapons if we can only use them. Is it not really a ridiculous fact that of all our modern dramatists none, (for who can reckon Mr. Rowe now a days?) has approached in any degree to the form of play delivered to us by the founders of our stage. All—from Massinger & Shirley down to Shiel & Knowles more or less French: and how could they expect a lasting or a real popularity? The people are in this case wiser than the critics: instinct and habit a truer guide than the half & half learning & philosophy of ramblers, quarterlys, and magaziners.

Poor Mr. professor Milman will really be quite horrified, if he should live to read the J. book, at the thought that a fellow of so villainous a school as its author should have been bred up at Oxford during his poetical dictatorship there. I hope he will review me. Indeed I only lament that so much absurdity in reviews is likely to escape me on account of my foreign residence.

Luz is an excellent joke: but tell me if I do not write too irreligiously for Cautland, I am so accustomed to German professors & rationalist theologians, who come into public places & say that they do not wish to be considered as Christians that I have quite forgotten the proper respect for the tenderness of those elect souls who are determined that God shall damn their unconverted neighbours & and help him a little as far as lies in their power in this life. I like candour very well, but do not see the fun of being a martyr. Si populus vult decipi, decipiatur.

For the rest, the play is too long, the first Act somewhat in Briton Chief(62) style, the 2ⁿᵈ dull & undramatic, the 3 latter better in all respects, so begin with 3ʳᵈ Scene 3ʳᵈ Act if you want to read to the end without being greatly bored. There are too many songs & two of them are bad, somewhat Moorish and sentimental. Weakness you will find in the 2ⁿᵈ & beginning part of 3ʳᵈ scene of 4ᵗʰ act. A sweet but tedious sop for the admirers of the pretty I have thrown in at Scene 3 of Act V. but if I err not you have somewhere found among my MSS a sort of dying glorification of a young lady wh. is better and just fitted for the occasion. My Friend Isbrand I recommend to your attention: he's a nice fellow.

As to the Deaths I am doubtful. Procter will abuse their song as vulgar & will be right, but Death is a vulgar dog: and not admissible at any other court than Duke & Fool Isbrand's. I thought of making Isbr. allude to Goethe & Chateaubriand when he proposes to make his new fool, minister, but the former must not be even in jest ridiculed by any one who has a sense of his very great and various merits. By the way his Faust as he wrote it has been played lately & with great success at Brunswick. A hint to those who think that good & stirring poetry will be rejected by the public: for the Germans (vide Kotzebue, & the robbers,) have more taste for melodrama & that right prosy than our good bloody minded cocknies. But then the patents, the patents! To them we are indebted for our dramatic desertedness, for the translations from the French, for Beasly's Operas, Peake's comedies, and the Chief's tragedy.

I have been lately reading the comedies of Holberg(63) the Dane, of whom his own countrymen & many Germans speak so highly, altho Schiller talks of the filth and ribaldry into which H. sinks, & Schlegel speaks of the atmosphere of his plays as one in which "there pours down continually a heavy shower of cudgels." These two good latter people have only read the elder German translation wʰ was good for nothing. Holberg writes with a great deal of humour, draws character rudely, but decisively, & the Danes are right to be proud of him. Another living Dane, Ingemann,(64) has written two very good W. Scottish historical novels—on subjects out of his national history—

My Russian is a very curious clever & learned fellow without a farthing in the world or the talent to make it & has dug up a great deal of interesting matter relative to the Hebrew doctrine of immortality. The King of Bavaria is just going to publish the first volume of his poetical works: he is a man of taste, talent & rational views, of course catholic.

Fr. Schlegel died lately at Dresden suddenly: he & his wife, a daughter of *Mendelssohn*! had both embraced the catholic religion: he lived in Vienna. Wrote proclamations for Francis I. & Metternich, & apologies for the Jesuits, his lectures on the philosophy of history must be therefore amusing. Mülliner *the Guilty*, has just published a tragedy in which he & Cotta the bookseller are the principal characters. A very washy poet Dr Raupach(51) is the most fertile dramatic writer in Germany now a days he is at Berlin: a thing brought out at Cov.: Garden last year was a not acknowledged translation of his Isidor & Olga—'twas called the "Serf."

Shakspeare was not wrong in letting Antigonus be shipwrecked in Bohemia. Valdemar the IInd of Denmark called the victorious fetched his wife Margaretha daughter of the King of Bohemia by water from Prague. We have only to read Elbe instead of seas, for I suppose one may be shipwrecked very well in a river: at all events the Elbe is good enough for a stage shipwreck. My motto in correspondence is, you are aware, "no trust!" if you don't answer I don't rejoice—I have used some of the Last man for the end of Fool's Trag: as you will see—T. L. B. Shall I review the King of Bavaria & send him to some paper?

Addressed to
    T. F. Kelsall Esq
        Fareham
        Hants

To Bryan Waller Procter
19ᵗʰ April, 1829

My dear Procter,—Accept my thanks for the patience and attention with which you have read my M.S., and for the manner in which you have spoken of it. I fear that if you had expressed your disapprobation of some of it still more strongly, I should have been obliged to confess that you were right. If you, as I have cause to apprehend, are not too well engaged in other and more substantial pursuits, you would oblige me still more by specifying the scenes and larger passages which should be erased (that is to say, if I am to let any considerable part remain as it is, for perhaps it might take less time to enumerate such bits as might be retained?). For the three classes of defects which you mention— obscurity, conceits, and mysticism,—I am afraid I am blind to the first and last, as I may be supposed to have associated a certain train of ideas to a certain mode of expressing them, and my four German years may have a little impaired my English style; and to the second I am, alas! a little partial, for Cowley was the first poetical writer whom I learned to understand. I will, then, do my best for the Play this summer; in the autumn I return to London, and then we will see what can be done. I confess to being idle and careless enough in these matters, for one reason, because I often very shrewdly suspect that I have no real poetical call.

I would write more songs if I could, but I can't manage rhyme well or easily. I very seldom get a glimpse of the right sort of idea in the right light for a song; and eleven out of the dozen are always good for nothing. If I could rhyme well and order complicated verse harmoniously, I would try odes; but it's too difficult.

Am I right in supposing that you would denounce and order to be rewritten all the prose scenes and passages?— almost all the first and second, great part of the third act.

Much of the two principal scenes of the fourth and fifth to be strengthened, and its opportunities better worked on. But you see this is no trifle, though I believe it ought to be done.

Can you tell me whether Vondel's "Lucifer" has been translated? It is a tragedy somewhat in the form of Seneca. J. von Vondel was born in Cologne, 1587 (according to Van Rampen), and "Lucifer" published in 1654. Milton, born in 1608, published "Paradise Lost" 1667.

It is to me very unlikely that Milton should have been acquainted with the Dutch language in Holland long after this period, and M was Cromwell's Latin secretary; therefore, if he had any business with the Dutch, he would not have transacted it unnecessarily in their language, and I do not recollect that he visited Holland in his travels; if he had, he would hardly have gone farther than learned Leyden. Both on this account and because I am rather partial to Holland and the Dutch (for their doings against Spain, their toleration, their (old) liberty of the press, and their literature wonderfully rich for so small a people), I was very much pleased and struck on finding two lines in Vondel's "Lucifer," which I translate literally:

> "*And rather the first prince at an inferior court,*
> *Than in the blessed light the second or still less.*"
> "Lucifer." Act II

Does it not seem as if at certain periods of the world some secret influence in nature was acting universally on the spirit of mankind, and predisposing it to the culture of certain sciences or arts, and leading it to the discovery even of certain special ideas and facts in these? I do not know whether the authors of philosophies of history have as yet made this observation, but it is sufficiently obvious, and might be supported by numerous instances. So in our times Scheele and Priestly; the former in Sweden a few weeks later than P. discovered oxygen gas. A little time before we have half-a-dozen candidates for the title of appliers of the power of steam in mechanics, etc. Middleton's "Witch" and "Macbeth" present in the lyrical parts so close a similarity, that one can hardly doubt of the existence here of imitation on one side. I cannot but think that M. was the plagiarist, and that some error must have occurred with regard to the dates of the two pieces.

The King of Bavaria has commenced poet, and a very sorry one he appears to be from the newspaper extracts. Kings as well as cobblers should keep to their craft—and Louis is a very reputable king; but still every inch a king, as you may see from his having made Thorwaldsen a Knight of the Bavarian Crown!

That you may see that I am not the only careless dramatist going, I quote you three lines from Oehlenschläger's new play, the "Norseman in Constantinople." "Ha!" his great, strapping tragic hero says in rage and despair:

> *"Ha! knew the porkers what the old boar suffers,*
> *They would raise up a dismal grunt and straight*
> *Free him from torture."*

This is as literally translated as possible; and do not disbelieve me if it should not happen to be in the German translation, which, of course, is more likely to be in London than the Danish original. I have it from the latter; probably it is not in the German, which I have not seen. Moreover, Oehlenschläger is one of the very first of continental dramatists, perhaps the first, far above Müller, Grillparzer, Raupach, Immermann, etc. I will sacrifice my raven to you; but my crocky is really very dear to me; and so, I dare say, was Oehlenschläger's pig-sty metaphor to him.

Yours ever
T. L. Beddoes.

To Thomas Forbes Kelsall
April the last^e
Göttingen 29, [1829]

My dear Kelsall,—You will probably by this time have heard from Procter & Bourne the decision of the higher powers with regard to Isbrand & his peers: the play is to be revised & improved. The whole summer therefore will be occupied in this business & in the autumn on my return to town we will finally revise and consult with the booksellers &c. I have requested Procter, if he can find time, to specify his objections, and as soon as he has done that I shall do the same by you—

What you have brought forward is, I believe, quite right & shall be adopted. With regard to the ruling unamiability of the prominent characters, the weakness of the women &c you are right: and here also I have hit upon an important improvement as it appears just now to me, wh. I think you will approve. Instead of some weak Balaam two page scenes I will introduce a formal wooing of Amala by Adalmar, which she shall gently but pretty firmly decline: he shall then be supported by the arguments & authority of her father, the dull old gentleman: Amala shall then declare herself most peremptorily against it & appeal to Adalmar's generosity: he will give her up honourably, but it must appear that they are really or going to be married for the purpose of bettering Athulf by means of this disappointment and his contrition.

After this the Cain & Abel scene will tell better—it shall be ameliorated & curtailed. The other lady can hardly be brought much more forward—Having lost her love in the first act she would be infinitely tedious in the four latter—but her scene of meeting with the raised up Wolfram which really is capable of being rendered perhaps the finest in a poetical point of view is to be rewritten, wh. you will find necessary.

The charge of monotony in character is well grounded, but I can hardly do anything in this case, for the power of drawing character & humour—two things absolutely indispensable for a good dramatist, are the two first articles in my deficiencies: and even the imaginative poetry I think you will find in all my verse always harping on the same two or three principles: for which plain & satisfactory reasons I have no business to expect any great distinction as a writer: being allowed to be better than what is absolutely bad, & not quite an imitator is not enough for any lasting celebrity.

Read only an act of Shakespear, a bit of Milton, a scene or two of the admirably true Cenci, something of Webster, Marston, Marlowe or in fact anything deeply, naturally, sociably felt and then take to these Jestbooks—you will feel at once how forced, artificial, insipid, &c. &c. all such things are. To keep me up, you must be a daily reader of Walker, Sheele and the Lit Gaz. Parnassians. Believe me its only just now for want of a better, and that better or those dozen betters will rise whenever the public should favour this class of productions: they are in England beyond a doubt but opportunity whose merit is great too, has not and probably will not call them forth Procter has denounced the carrion crows—I can spare them: but he has also as "absolutely objectionable" anathematized Squats on a toadstool, with its crocodile; which I regard as almost necessary to the vitality of the piece.

What say you? If a majority decide against it, I am probably wrong. If you say it is nonsense—I and Isbrand reply that we meant it to be so: and what were a Fool's Trag: without a tolerable portion of nonsense. I thought it consistent with the character and scene and in its small way, and in comparison with the other minor merits of the play a set off like the nonsense of Wagner in Marlowe's, and the Monkies (not monkey: cats as some translators say,) in Goethe's Faustus—not to speak of higher nonsense in higher compositions.

Here is something of old Walther von der Vogelweide who wrote in the earlier part of the 13th century, but in his old German it is infinitely better

Under the lime tree on the daisied ground
  Two that I know of made this bed
There you may see heaped and scattered round
  Grass and blossoms broken and shed,
    All in a thicket down in the dale;
Tandaradei—sweetly sang the nightingale.
Ere I set foot in the meadow already
  Some one was waiting for somebody;
There was a meeting—Oh! gracious lady,
  There is no pleasure again for me.
    Thousands of kisses there he took,
Tandaradei—see my lips, how red they look.
Leaf and blossom he had pulled and piled
  For a couch, a green one, soft and high ,
And many a one hath gazed and smiled
  Passing the bower and pressed grass by:
    And the roses crushed hath seen,
Tandaradei, where I laid my head between;
  In this love-passage if any one had been there,
  How sad and shamed should I be;
    But -what -were we a doing alone among the
      green there
No soul shall ever know except my love and me,
  And the little nightingale
  Tandaradei—she, I wot, will tell no tale.

The King of Bavaria has not yet published: but very flat
specimens of his royal highness, his muse, have appeared in
the papers
    I must now send to the post
                           Yours truly
                              T. L. B.

Addressed to
    T. F. Kelsall Esqre
        Fareham
          Hants
            England

To Thomas Forbes Kelsall
Wurzburg 2 District N° 110
[Postmark] 19 July 1830

My dear Kelsall,—Your letter finds me at leizure (sic) (excuse all misspellings, my mother tongue begins to fade away in my memory and I was just going to write this word analogically like pleasure) and I will reply to, though perhaps not answer it. All about the play annoys me because I have utterly neglected it and feel not the least inclination to take any further trouble in the matter: however perhaps I may try this season, it cannot be printed this summer, and in autumn perhaps something may be done. This indifference is of itself almost enough to convince me that my nature is not that of one, who is destined to achieve anything very important in this department of literature; another is a sort of very moderate somewhat contemptuous respect for the profession of a mere poet in our inky age.

You will conceive that such a feeling accords well with, and perhaps results from a high delight in, first rate creators and illustrators of the creation as Æschylus, Shak. &c and a cordial esteem for those who, as highly polished moderns, have united their art with other solid knowledge & science, or political activity—Camoens, Dante & lower down many French and English accomplished rhymers;—and now Goethe, Tieck &c.

In the third place a man must have an exclusive passion for his art, and all the obstinacy and self denial wh: is combined with such a temperament, an unconquerable and all enduring will always working forwards to the only goal he knows; such a one must never think that there is any human employment so good (much less suspect that there may be not a few better,) so honourable for the exercise of his faculties, ambition, industry—and all those impolitic and hasty virtues which helped Icarus to buckle on his plumes and w^h we have left sticking in the pages of Don Quixote.

I am even yet however seriously of the opinion that it is ornamental and honourable to every nation and generation of mankind if they cherish among their numbers men of cultivated imagination capable of producing new and valuable works of art; and if I were soberly and mathematically convinced of my own genuineness (*inspiration* as the ancients w^d say) I might possibly, tho' I *won't promise*, find spirit and stability enough to give up my time to the cultivation of literature.

If dreams were dramatic calls as in the days or nights of Æschylus I might plead something too—He, according to Athenæus, sleeping in a vineyard, probably after acting a part in some Thespian satyric dialogue, had a vision of Bacchus descending to him and bidding him arise and write tragedies. The author of Agamemnon had a good right to relate such a nocturnal visit, if it had been paid to him, or even to invent it if a less divine nightmare had invited him to mount his hobby horse. We will not ask how many have won in this or any other lottery and the number they saw in their slumbers. I in my bed in Wurzburg did dream that I bought in an old bookshop for a small moiety of copper money, a little old dirty, dogs-eared, well-thumbed book and thereon in great agitation and joy saw at the first glance into the dialogue ('twas a playbook,) that it contained half-a-dozen genuine and excellent unknown plays, wh: no one could have written whose name and nature was not W. S.

To return to reality I will say then that I will try to write over again this last unhappy play, tho' I have no appetite to the task, and then I w^d wish to have it printed with any other little things that you may have and think worth printers ink because a second edition is not to be thought of, and any consequent poetical publication of mine very improbable. It is good to be tolerable or intolerable in any other line but Apollo defend us from brewing all our lives at a quintessential pot of the smallest ale Parnassian; such hope or memory is little soothing for any one whose mind is not quite as narrow as a column of eights and sixes.

I sometimes wish to devote myself exclusively to the

study of anatomy & physiology in science, of languages, and dramatic poetry, and have nothing to hinder me except— unsteadiness and indolence: wh. renders it extremely probable if not absolutely certain that I shall never be anything above a very moderate dabbler in many waters: if another very different spirit does not come over me very very soon you will do well to give me up. Indifference grows upon us and that renders my case very desperate.

Once more about the crocodile song—I have sent Bourne another song instead of it about an old ghost; one in the place of the 2nd song of the bridal serenaders, w^h was very commonplace and ought to have been abused by you, tho' I put these three purposely together, one something Moorish in rhythmus and expression, not equal to him (his song style is the best *false* one I know and glitters like broken glass—or he calls us and will show us a beautiful prospect in heaven or earth, gives us a tube to look thro' which looks like a telescope, and is a kaleidoscope—) but a tolerable watery imitation—the 2nd a specimen of the bad but very popular sentimental if—oh! and why? lovesong, and the 3rd in the style w^h to my conviction is the right and genuine one in tone, feeling and form for a song of the tender and more poetic kind.

No critic however will see what I meant & indeed I may have failed in my purpose, for Bourne seemed to like the I st as well as the 3rd I do not know whether I have written to you about song-writing, it is almost the only kind of poetry of w^h I have attained a decided and clear critical theory; in some letter either to you or Bourne I said a good deal about it; but what need of it? You have Shak: and the dramatists, Herrick, Suckling &c and know what I mean.

It is not easy to write a song with ease, tenderness, and that ethereal grace w^h you find among these writers. &c &c &c. Tieck's tale "Dichter-leben" in Urania 5 or 6 relates more to Marloe than Shakspeare. Tho this latter and Kit's crony Robert Green contribute their groats worth of wit to illustrate his repentance: and Nash is there too and Hemings in good keeping. I don't know whether it's translated—is William Lovell by the same among your novels from the

German, a capital thing: indeed T[*ieck*] is always clever but has studied so much in the old English and Spanish school that he is scarcely to be called popular among his country men tho' everywhere acknowledged and dreaded. I have learned much from his writings, from him and Wieland more than [*from*] any German writer.

Some prejudice or other kept me a long while from reading anything of Kleists, because I had somewhere read a vile magazine Translation of his "Spring" and I hate poems about the seasons: the other day I took up his "Käthchen von Heilbronn"—a chivalrous play, and was very agreeably surprized—my criticism is never worth much touching poetry of a loftier character—but I confess I am inclined to look upon Kleist as a person of very great talent for the romantic drama, there is evidently an inoculation from the Shakspearian vein in the piece, and a nature & simplicity w^h sends howling the pompous pasteboard affectations of Müllner, Raupach and other Calibans who lick the shoe of Gries's translated Calderon. His prince of Homberg and other works I have not yet read, altho' I really believed a week ago that I was acquainted with everything worth reading in German belles lettres from the Niebelingenlied down to Tiecks last novel.

How is it possible that it could have escaped your tact for the drama, that the 1st act of D^s J. B. must end with the last words of Wolfram, all the rest being superfluous and derogatory? You will see it clearly if you look into the scene again and draw your pen through all the Ahs and Ohs and HMs w^h follow.

You have never any of you said a word about the preface —is it to be printed or not? I think better not—it is ill-written and contains nothing new excepting the quotation from Bilderdijk w^h I prize highly as the historical vindication of the Shakspearian form, and therefore a decisive refutation of all application of Aristotelian maxims to our drama for those who require an authority besides that of the feelings of the people. I believe I shall leave the crocodile where he is: and put the "old ghost" into the shoes of Adam & Eve about whom I care nothing: and I prefer being anonymous as aforesaid.

I hardly venture to open my M.S.; I read Shakspeare, and Wordsworth, the only English books I have here, and doubt —and seem to myself a very Bristol diamond, not genuine, altho' glittering just enough to be sham.

Wurzburg is one of the oldest universitys in Germany—a very clever prof, of Medicine, and capital Midwife brought me here and a princely hospital—Franconian wines are mostly white. Stein, Leisten, Gressen are the best; Wurzb. lies amidst vine covered hills, and the Maine flows away at a considerable breadth—I stay till August's end—then perhaps to Florence so you had better write before that time

T. L. B

Bourne tells me that Dr. Satan Montgomery has been buffeted by Macaulay in the Ed:; glad of it, altho' such critical works have forfeited their authority in consequence of their vile mistakes. Do people read Ld Byron still as they used to— or is Montgom: really his successor? Have you not read Pelham &c?

I have made a mistake about Kleist. There are 2 German Boets of the name. Christian Ewaldo K. born 1715 died of the wounds he received at ye battle of Kunnersdorf in Frederick great's army Aug. 24 1759. wrote The *Spring* &c. Heinrich von K. the dramatist committed suicide in partnership with Mrs. Adolphine Sophia Henricke Vogel in a wood near Potsdam Novr 21. 1811.

Tieck has translated the 2nd Maidens Trag: and attributes it to Massinger, I must ask him why? the poisoning and painting is somewhat like him but also like Cyril Tourneur— & it is too imaginative for old Philip.

95

Addressed to
   T. F. Kelsall Esqre
    Fareham
     Hants
      England

LETTER XXXII

To Thomas Forbes Kelsall
   Wurzurg No. 186
   1 District
   [*Postmark 10 Jan 1831*]

My dear Kelsall,—Another winter in Wurzburg: I do not kno[*w*] when I shall summon courage enough to return to your deuced dear Island. You might have written to me before this as you have now matter enough in the Gun-Powder-Plot, of which our literary periodicals speak so mysteriously that I am totally at a loss whether it be a merry political hoax, of which the Germans have as yet no conception, or a serious Irelandiad: and then the sixpenny old dramatists.

I have some idea of raising my ghost (in the never ending D's J. B.) at the close of the 5th act, and amalgamating the last scene of the third with the last of the 5th the 1st act must then be cut in two w^h is practicable enough—but then I am at a loss for business and a good blow at the end of the 3rd. And a play in four acts is a cripple. Either three or 5.

In the first the deed must be committed the consequences of w^h employ the following: in the second a reaction attempted and a second seed sown for ripening in the after-time: in the third, which needs not to be the most powerful as I once thought, the storm gathers, doubts rise, or the termination w^h appears to be at hand is intercepted by some bold and unexpected invention, a new event the development of a character, hitherto obscure, a new resolve &c gives a new turn to the aspect of the future: in the fourth all is consummated, the truth is cleared up, the final determination taken, the step of Nemesis is heard: and in the fifth the atonement follows.

The first, fourth and fifth must be most attractive and interesting from the confliction of passions and the events occasioned by them: the 2 is a pause for retrospection, anticipation; in the third is rather the struggle between the will of man and the moral law of necessity w^h awaits inevitably his past actions—the pivot of all tragedy. I have really begun a little to alter the ill-fated play in question. What do you say to a drinking song like this at the beginning of the present 2nd act? I am not in the least satisfied with it?— On second thoughts I will not bore you with it—indeed it is utterly useless to send you anything, for you always forget to criticize, and abuse properly w^h it is the duty of every friend to do as long as the confided piece remains in M.S. Otherwise you sh^d have observed how stupid and superfluous almost all the 2nd act of J B is how commonplace the 2nd bridal song in the 4th &^{o} &^{o} ad infinitum.

You may give me credit for carelessness, if you will not for want of superabundant vanity (a spice is necessary & self-esteem the wise it call); it is 8 years since I have published anything, & how long will it be before I am again under the press? heaven knows—I think the reading populace ought to be much obliged to me for my forbearance: 'tis a pity that other young rhyming gents are not equally economical of their tediousness, Campbell is really a good example—or would be but I fear his poverty & not his will consented. Leopold Schefer(65), a good novelist, proposes, for the purpose of resuscitating the drama to return to the custom of the Greeks, i.e. to keep all Theatres closed through the greater part of the year and to open them during a few holiday-weeks once in 3 years, I think at Easter, Christmas &c , for the representation of plays for a prize—a good chimæra.

Many things are quite absurd and destructive of all poetry

in arrangements w^h appear not of the slightest consequence. I am convinced that playbills for instance are very pernicious; one should never know the actors names and private circumstances, the spectators would then be compelled to identify them with their dramatic characters, the interest w^d be much purer and undivided, the illusion carried as far as it can & ought to be—how can people enter deeply into the spirit of a tragedy for instance—in comedy it is a matter of less consequence, whose question is, how do you like Kean to-night? Is not Claremont delightful in Rosenkranz? etc.—Othello & Richard & Rosenkranz are here obliged to play Claremont & Kean instead of the reverse.

The actor on the other hand deprived of his private name & existence must feel more convinced of the reality of his 5-act life, would be liberated from the shackles of timidity & the temptations of individual vanity, w^d [*grow*] careless about his creditors & be unable to try & please the lady's as Mr. with the handsome leg &c. wink to his friends in the pit &c &c. To whet curiosity and occasion astonishment is not the least important object of the dramatist; the actors might have learned from Scott that anonymous mysteriousness is one of the most effective arts for this purpose—A distant idea of the use of this concealment probably caused the custom observed in the announcement of a new play—principal characters by Messrs Doe & Roe—but the names of the people in the drama ought to be printed with the necessary key [father, son &c] not those of the gentleman who lodges at the pastry cooks, wears the threadbare coat, &c.

The Greeks (from whom we can learn much if we understand their motives—) were in possession of this secret, and this is the real meaning of their masks, wh. have so much bothered the critics; and these were doubly useful, they deceived to a certain degree not only the spectator, but also the actor with the semblance of an heroic and unknown person, and prevented the annoying familiarity of the people on the stage. Of course I do not wish to see these sort of masks on our stage—(our passionate drama renders them impossible —though it might be an interesting experiment to try them once in an adaptation of Agamemnon, the Bacchæ,

Antigone or Electra—to conclude with the satyric Drama—
the Cyclops:) it is only to be lamented that we have no other
means of completely disguising our actors and making
Richard, Hamlet, Macbeth—as absolutely distinct and
independent individuals—as Œdipus & Orestes must have
been—the Athenians w^d I am sure have pelted their fellow
citizen and neighbour as the pathetic hobbling, ulcerous
Philoctetes off the stage with onions, only a conviction of his
reality could have reconciled their frivolous imagination with
him or subdued them to compassion—and Agamemnon or
Hercules unmasked would have been saluted with their
nicknames from all sides.

    Othello's colour is a sort of mask, & this is a reason
perhaps why Shak: has given him so much less ideal
language and more simple household truth than his other
characters, the whole play is barer of imagery than any other
of his, except the musicians with their silver sound there is
no conductor for laughter from the tragic characters; Sh:
seems really to intend more illusion than elsewhere, & is not
the purpose gained?

    The witches, Peter & the nurse, the gravediggers &
Polonius, in a less degree Kent & Lear's Fool, are all more or
less purposely destructive of the tragic illusion—give time to
recover from the surprize wh the course of the events
produce[s]: their good is that they give the hearer to
understand that the poet is not absolutely in earnest with his
deaths & horrors & leaves it to them to be affected with them
or not as they think proper, and secondly, that the audience,
as well as every body, is much less inclined to laugh at &
deride the gravity of a person, with whom his wit & satire has
compelled them to laugh—besides that the change is
grounded on the law of oscillation w^h pervades all physical
and moral nature—sleeping and waking (merriment & tears),
sin & repentance, life & death, w^h all depend & are
consequent on one another.

    So much for my dramaturgic ideas on playbills, I do not
know that any one else has fallen on them—what do you
think of them as theory? The pause between the acts—w^h the
Greeks and Sh: I believe did not allow—is another dangerous

innovation: the thread of events is interrupted, one talks to one's neighbour, hears news and forgets the fictitious in the real events, the state of mind produced by the opening is altered, and as soon as we are with difficulty brought back to the track over w^h the poet w^d lead us another interruption undoes all again. The actors in the meantime chat behind the scenes, Cordelia flirts with her papa, Arthur makes King John a pigtail, Constance comforts herself with a cup of tea, Juliet dances with the dead Mercutio and all such things occur w^h breed familiarity & carelessness and damp the excited imagination, cool the ardour of the players.

These & some other apparently trifling things have, I am convinced done the drama much more harm, rendered it less poetical, and spoiled the audience & performers, than the innocent dogs, & horses, who act always better than the bipeds & w^h are as allowable as painted houses &c. Agamemnon's chariot was drawn by real horses I doubt not, Shakespeare made a good use of his friend's dog who played Lance &c &c. I acknowledge that licences, patents, theatrical censure &c have been far more noxious; the stage must be as free as the press before anything very good comes again. But these things w^h I point out can easily be removed, others probably not before the abolition of tithes, corn bill &c.

If parliament had nothing to do of greater consequence, Ld Melbourne who dabbled in Drury lane theatricals might do something for us & I wish some one w^d publicly remind him of the subject. Tiecks continuation of Dichterleben is a delightful explanation of Shakespeares life & sonnets, I suppose it is already translated somewhere: it appeared in his Novellenkranz Taschenbuch Aug. 1831.

Adieu & answer & send me the song and death scene you spoke of; you are lazy enough & cannot complain of me unless you improve. I wish you w^d tell me what things of Tiecks are translated as I should wish to introduce him to the English as he deserves. I think he w^d be & know he ought to be much more relished than Goethe who after all is only a name in England—it is a confounded bore & baulked me much that I have no connection with any publisher or journalist in England—I sh^d then have some stimulus &c—do

some good, now I can do nothing—

T.L. B.

I leave Wurzburg in March: destination uncertain.

Addressed to
        T. F. Kelsall Esq.
            Fareham
                Hants
                    England

Wurzburg May 4th 1831

After promising to subscribe £5 towards the subscription for the support of candidates who were professed supporters of the Reform Bill:—

LETTER XXXIII (Fragment)

To Revell Phillips
Wurzburg May 1832

We have been fortunate enough at W: to have entertained a considerable number of the most distinguished Polish officers and other exiles from that unconquered, tho' at present enslaved, country, among others Rybinsky, Dembinski, Stanislaus Astrowski with his 3 sons, and we expect Malachowski daily: Saxony, Bavaria, and the other smaller states of Southern Germany have done much to obliterate the stain, which the perfidious conduct of the Prussian government have attached to the German name: but I am afraid that the Polish and European people will not

101

be very ready to forget and forgive the pitiable imbecility of France and the temporising selfishness of England in this matter. Every Bavarian carried a joke on the new king of Greece in his heart, many a one on his tongue.

LETTER XXXIV (Fragment)

To Revell Phillips
Strasburg Septr 25th 1832

The absurdity of the King of Bavaria has cost me a good deal, as I was obliged to oppose every possible measure to the arbitrary illegality of his conduct, more for the sake of future objects of his petty royal malice than my own, of course in vain.

P.S. By the way I have taken an M.D. at Wurzburg but do not at present desire to make use of the title.

LETTER XXXV (Fragment)

To Revell Phillips
Zurich 1833 Decr 18th

My dear Phillips,—I beg you to present my best compliments to Mrs. R. Phillips for her kind message: I am afraid our friend Kelsall was guilty of putting me into the Athenæum(66). It is of as little consequence as possible, but curious enough that those lines of which I imagined that I had burnt the only copy some years ago in Gottingen, should nevertheless have gained the light of letter press in London. I wish they had been more worthy of it.

With all deference to the opinion of Mrs. R. Phillips and all thank's for her kind partiality, I cannot help thinking that every able bodied person, capable of what's called tuning the lyre to all manner of ballads &c who spares the much annoyed reading public his possible and impossible productions, is entitled to some sort of acknowledgment for his rare forbearance.

I believe that the London publishers are extremely unwilling to publish translations of foreign medical works: nevertheless I should wish much to know whether no one would undertake the printing of one which is destined to appear at Easter, Schoenlien's(67) Natural History of the diseases of Europeans—it will consist of about 6 vols of which 1 or 2 will come out in the Spring—Sch: is perhaps the most distinguished of German Physicians, (now professor here, banished by that ingenious Jack-a-napes of Bavaria) & his work is destined to attract the attention of the medical men of all nations.

I know both him and German, and should wish to render the literature of my country a service by translating the book —for the MSS of the first volume I would require nothing but cannot afford anything more than the trouble. I know that the book must be sooner or later Englished, I do not expect that any book seller will take my offer and so in the end it will be done like most of the Anglo-German things of the kind by some one only half acquainted with the language as an exercise.

LETTER XXXVI (Fragment)

To Revell Phillips
Zwich Feby 27. 1834

I shall wish on my return to England to have a pretty decent sum of money for the purchase of books, in specie, foreign ones, and other expensive materials of a medical life: furniture &c &c for German books alone I shall have need of some hundreds. In spite of all the stupidity of medical booksellers & of the insular and insolent self sufficiency of their authors and readers in England I shall translate Schoenlien and, if I cannot otherwise get it printed, publish it at my own expense. The apparent imprudence of this resolution will be amply vindicated after some years. Since the time of Boerhaave no work, not even excepting Cullen, has appeared

LETTER XXXVII (Fragment)

To Revell Phillips
Zurich May 12th 1834

I am not sure whether I shall repair to Paris or return to England—probably the latter, since Russia advances with so hasty strides towards the Alps from whence then she will cast her withering shade over the whole Continent.

LETTER XXXVIII (Fragment)

To Revell Phillips
Zurich March 4ᵗʰ 1835

I suppose it is only a joke of Mr. Bourne's that he hints of having heard from some acquaintance of mine that I had taken a house here was become professor &c stories which I only request you to contradict if you should happen to meet with gossipers on so insignificant subjects, because the latter assertion might tend to awaken expectations which the degree of my scientific knowledge could only ultimately disappoint. As I can conceive nothing more hostile to honest success, it is utterly contrary to my intention; if any one should imagine that I am more than I am, and it would be much more ingenious if such as have leisure to speculate on my merits would endeavour to turn the telescope of their imaginations and try to think me less—excuse my dear sir this egotism but no one likes to be written down an ass in golden capitals.

LETTER XXXIX (Fragment)

To Revell Phillips
Zurich Septʳ 14 1835

I have been since the end of June here where I shall probably not become professor. Schoenlien proposed me as such to the medical faculty of the University and the latter unanimously seconded him. The board of education however objected to the nomination, inasmuch as a very reasonable regulation requires that every Professor of the University shall have either published some scientific work or officiated somewhere as teacher. This rule they are naturally disinclined to transgress and I to write, having nothing new to communicate or to have the trouble of lecturing, without a collection of specimens, [*which*] would be to no purpose and indeed impracticable.

LETTER XL

To Thomas Forbes Kelsall
Zurich chez M. Waser Neustadt
[*Postmark*] *9 March 1837*

My dear Kelsall,—I am preparing for the press, as the saying is, among other graver affairs, a volume(68) of prosaic poetry and poetical prose. It will contain half a dozen Tales, comic, tragic, and dithyrambic, satirical and semi-moral: perhaps half a hundred lyrical Jewsharpings in various styles and humours: and the stillborn D.J.B. with critical and cacochymical remarks on the European literature, in specie the hapless dramas of our day.

I am not asinine enough to imagine that it will be any very great shakes, but what with a careless temper and the pleasant translunary moods I walk and row myself into upon the lakes and over the alps of Switzerland it will, I hope, turn out not quite the smallest ale brewed out with the water of the fountain of ye horse's foot.

Now then, I write to beg you, as the saying is, to send me in a letter a copy of a certain scene and song w^h you, being the possessor of the only existing MS. thereof once proposed as an amelioration of one in D's J. B. This affair will be very much cut down, a good many faults corrected; a little new matter added to it: and the whole better arranged. But I can hardly consent to eradicate my crocodile song, wh. you

106

know, B. C. and all persons of proper feeling, as the saying is, strongly condemned. After all I only print it because it is written and can't be helped and really only for such readers as the pseudonymical lawyer mentioned, W. Savage L[*andor*]: yourself etc.! (if there be yet a plural number left). G. D.(69) appears to me to have grown deuced grey, whether it be the greyness of dawn, of life's evening twilight, or of a nascent asinine metempsychosis I cannot distinguish at this distance.

As a specimen I send you a bit of foolery and a snack of fine feeling, and if you don't answer me before June I shall let another rhymed bore loose at you: or what will be as bad, I hope a few of my anatomical discoveries and physiological fancies. I dare say you have been many years a happy married man: I am still Your unhappy humble servant, and the Lord knows singley and sinfully virtuous

T. L. B.

P.S here they are but they allude to passages in the tales containing 'em

> Has no one seen my heart of yore?
>   My heart bids run away;
> And if you catch him, ladies, do
>   Return him me, I pray.
> On earth he is no more I hear
>   Upon the land or sea
> For the women found the rogue so queer
>   They sent him back to me.
> In heaven there is no purchaser
>   For such strange ends and odds
> Says a Jew, who goes to Jupiter
>   To buy and sell old goods.
> So there is but one place more to search,
>   That's not genteel to tell
> Where demonesses go to church,—
>   So Xtians fair, farewell.

I think of thee at daybreak still,
    And then thou art my playmate small
Beside our strawroofed village rill
    Gathering cowslips tall,
And chasing oft the butterfly,
    Wh. flutters past like treacherous life.

You smile at me and at you I,
    A husband boy & baby wife
    I think of thee at noon again
And thy meridian beauty high
    Falls on my bosom like young rain
Out of a summer sky.
    And I reflect it in the tear
W^h 'neath thy picture drops forlorn
And then my love is bright & clear
& manlier than it was at morn.
I think of thee by evening's star,
    And softly, melancholy slow,
An eye doth glisten from afar
    All full of lovely woe.
The air then sighingly doth part
    And or from death the cold, or Love
I hear the passing of a dart,
    But hope and move & look above.

I think of thee at black midnight
And woe & agony it is
To see thy cheek so deadly white,
To hear thy graveworm hiss.*
But looking on thy lips is cheer.
They closed in love, pronouncing love.
And then I tremble, not for fear,
But in thy breath from heaven above.

Now if you wish to avoid any further similar visitation of doggrell you'd better take your quill from behind your ear and write and write and write like to a rat without a brief. Apropos of [*blank*] know that J. G. H. B.(70) has been poetizing, Novellizing, and magazinning a year or two &, by Haynes Bayly(71), better than your h^{ble} serv^t, as the saying is. But what is Hecuba to you? I dare say you've forgotten all such childishnesses as these, and you're then in the right on't, not so h^{ble} serv^t. But who can help being an ass as long as he must graze in ye vale of tears? That onion wisdom, wh preventeth transformation, (moly—allium Dioscorides. Sibthorpe—nigrum Sprengel if. Spr. Gesch. d. Botanik B^d n s 37. 68 n f u T. 2. ahem!) a'n't the potherb I fancy. A jew, a jew, a jew !

Remember me

T.L.B.

March 9, 1837

P.S I send this directed to Revell Phillips Esq. because I don't know your whereabouts but I suppose you're in England.

* No: he don't, no more nor a Bristol alderman at t'other turtle.— Ed. [*Bcddoes.*]

To Thomas Forbes Kelsall
[*Postmark*]
[*Zurich*]
May 15 [*1837*] *the hills*
covered with snow.
Temperature + 6° R

My dear Kelsall,—My best thanks for your prompt and agreeable answer. Your part of the letter being much more satisfactory than mine. I know not what the creator of a planet may think of his first efforts when he looks into the cavernous recesses which contain the first sketches of organized life beings,—but it is strange enough to see the fossilized faces of ones forgotten literary creatures years after the vein of feeling in wh. they were formed, has remained closed and unexplored.

I shall not be able to make much of the death scene, it is too diffuse and dithyrambic. Pray do not make too much of my productions: you go too far by much in talking of fashionable publishers and the spring season. Most probably I shall be reduced to print at my own expense, for no Oilier exists at present, I believe, and one can hardly expect to get rid of 100 copies by sale.

I know well that publishing at one's own cost is as promising a speculation, as that in Spanish bonds for a man who wishes to lose; but the work is so perfectly adapted to remain unread that it would be unfair to think of mulcting any unoffending bookseller to the necessary amount. At first I intended to have it printed by Baudry or Galignani at Paris or at Brussels: but it goes on so slowly in this cold and snowy weather that it may cost me much more time than I anticipated.

I w^d gladly send you copies of the four chapters, containing as many tales, finished, if I had any creature here capable of writing English, but I cannot endure copying what

I have myself written. I do not intend to publish or republish anything of an earlier date (except D. J. B). Pygmalion is, if I recollect aright, considerable trash, and what the devil is Alfarabi? Did you ever meet with the exile of Idria a narrative poem, by Bourne? I have not seen it—or Christ xfied by a reformed college aquaintance of mine, the rev^d W. E. Wall. I sh^d apprehend that the latter had exceeded in atrocity the rev^d Cleophas and the Pharisees.

I thank you sincerely for your kind invitation to Fareham, of w^h I think to avail myself one time or other. I have been staying all the winter here for the purpose of taking an extensive Alpine walk in July and August. It was my intention to have gone up to the top of several mountains w^h I have not yet visited, Pilate, the Titlis &c, but I fear that the great quantity of snow w^h has fallen in the winter and is still falling at this moment will hardly be so far melted by the sun of this summer, as yet powerless, as to leave the latter, a tallish fellow about 10700 feet above the level of ye sea, accessible to wingless bipeds; so I must even content myself with once more treading on the summits of my humbler acquaintance, Rigi, Faul & Seidelhorn etc. These summer excursions among the vallies, the glaciers and the mighty eminences of this magnificent countries are to me the most delightful of all relaxations, without w^h I sh^d be as dull and sour as the refuse whey, in w^h no pig has dipped his snout.

I am sorry to acknowledge that the later writings of Landor have not reached our subalpine region. So much the better, there will be something new for me when I return that I shall be able to read. Have you read Tieck's Shakespeare Novels (Dichterleben Th. I. u. 2.) and is W. S. L's Dearstealing(72) as true and worthy of its hero? T., a writer whom I prefer very much to the Goethe about whom the folks in y^r Isle, who manage to wade through his treacherous pages on the back of some square fat dictionary, are all gone stark staring, translating mad—T. Published a year or two ago in his Novellenkranz a biographical romance in w^h Camoens plays the principal part—w^h I prefer to his Shakspeare and hold to be the most perfect of his, and consequently of German *human* fictions. His dramatic poems, fairytales &c are I believe nearly unknown in your part of Europe.

But of this anon when I happen to be in your neighbourhood. Such matters are fitted for discourse over a tankard than one over the channel and across France. What are the votaries of the Muse doing yonder? What is Cosmo dei Medici?(73) Paracelsus? Strafford? and Sergeant Talfourd's Ion or John? You must know that Baudry and Galignani print little besides the fashionable novels, wh. I can seldom manage to read in spite of the most devoted application. Bulwer excepted, who is very entertaining, as long as he abstains from aspiring to a sublimer or more poetical sphere, than the very respectable one of pickpockets and lawyers—(I beg pardon) and old clothesmen.

My fingers are now so cold that I must put them into my pockets and sing you a very objectionable piece of foolery, enough to ruin the reputation of any one, who wishes to introduce his writings into good society—Allons! It's a sparkling piece of anecdote filed out of the golden Legend—and extracted from Chap V of the Ivory Gate—or lesser Dionysiacs— (my new book—)

THE NEW CECILIA.

Whoever has heard of St. Gingo
   must know that the gipsy,
   he married, was tipsy
every night of her life with old stingo:
and, after the death of St. Gingo,
    the wonders, he did do,
    his infidel widow
denied with unladylike lingo—
   "A parcel of nonsense together," &
   Tost Gingo a fig, and a feather end.
   "He no more can work wonder
   Then a clyster-pipe thunder
   or I sing a psalm with my nether end."
As she spoke it, her breakfast beginning on

a tankard of homebrewed inviting ale,
Lo! the part she was sitting & sinning on
struck the 100th
psalm up like a nightingale.
Loud as birds in an Indian forest, or
A mystic memnonian marble in
The desert at daybreak, that chorister
    breathed forth its Œolian warbling:

          *   *   *   *

Therefore, Ladies, repent & be sedulous
in praising your lords, lest, ah well a day!
a judgement befall the incredulous,
& their latter ends melt into melody.

    What stuff! I shall not give you any more extracts, for fear
of spoiling your appetite for the promised laughable mouse
in toto. To tell the truth however I prefer the above and such
like absurdity to your Pygmalion and contend that the
same is far more poetical. To be sure it is rather too much in
the style of Campbell, but hardly so entirely as fairly to
deserve the name of an imitation.
    You are desirous of knowing what my thoughts or
superstitions may be regarding things human, sub human,
and superhuman: or you wish to learn my habits, pursuits,
and train of life. Now as you have not me before you in the
witness's box, you must excuse my declining to answer
directly to such questioning. I will not venture on a
psychological self portraiture, fearing, and I believe with
sufficient reason, to be betrayed into affectation,
dissimulation, or some other alluring shape of lying. I believe
that all autobiographical sketches are the result of mere
vanity—not excepting those of St. Augustin & Rousseau—
falsehood in the mask & mantle of truth.
    Half ashamed and half conscious of his mendacious self-
flattery the historian of his own deeds, or geographer of his

own mind breaks out now and then indignantly and revenges himself on his own weakness by telling some very disagreeable truth of some other person, and then re-established in his own good opinion marches on cheerfully in the smooth path towards the temple of his own immortality. Yet even here you see I am indirectly lauding my own worship for not being persuaded to laud my own worship. How sleek, smooth tongued, paradisical a deluder art thou, sweet self conceit! Let great men give their own thoughts on their own thoughts: from such we can learn much: but let the small deer hold jaw and remember what the philosopher says, "fleas are not lobsters: damn their souls."

Without any such risk, however, I can tell you how I employ, or abuse, my time. You must know that I am an M.D of the U. of Wurzburg and possess a very passable knowledge of anatomy & physiology etc. that I narrowly escaped becoming professor of comparative Anat^y in the U. of Zurich, (having been recommended unanimously for that chair by the medical faculty here,) by means of a timely quarrel, in which I engaged more solito with several members of the government.

Now being independent & having all the otium, if not the dignitas eines privatisirenden Gelehrten, sometimes I dissect a beetle, sometimes an oyster, and very often trudge about the hills and the lakes, with a tinbox on my back, and "peep and botanize" in defiance of W. W. Sometimes I peep half a day through a microscope. Sometimes I read Italian (in w^h I am only a smatterer,) or what not, & not seldom drink I & smoke like an Ætna.

As sudden thunder,
    Pierces night,
As magic wonder,
    Wild affright,
Rives asunder
    Mens delight,
Our ghost, our corpse and we
    Cleave The Sea

114

As hath the lizard
     Serpent fell,
As goblin grizard
     From the spell
Of pale wizard
     Sinks to hell;
Our life, our laugh, our lay-
     Pass away.

As startle morning
     Trumpets bright,
As snowdrop scorning
     Winter's might
Rises warning
     Like a spright:
We buried dead and slain
     Rise again

And so I weave my Penelopean web and rip it up again: and so I roll my impudent Sisyphean stone; and so I eat my beefsteak, drink my coffee, and wear my coats out at elbow, and pay my bills (when I can,) as busy an humble bee, as any who doth nothing.

I hear and read not a jot about B. Cornwall. Two years ago when I visited your Island I left a horridly scribbled dirty old card at his chambers, which, as far as I know, was never returned. Now no one has behaved so frankly, kindly, and encouragingly to me as he did. He overrated my twopenny poetical talent as much as yourself, but exerted himself most disinterestedly; were it another cause I would say nobly in my favour.

I will some day or other show you his letter tome (1829) about the wretched fool's Tragedy, which is as candid as goodnatured, and wellwishing as man ever wrote. I sh^d be extremely sorry not to enjoy his acquaintance after my return to your island: but being a great wretch, a horrid radical & a person entirely unfitted for good society, I never wonder at my acquaintances disavowing [*or*] cutting me, as the Arabs & the English say. Don't care a zephyr as long as cash, good spirits, and foolery in brain.

Capital was my first adventure in 1835 at Dover. London Coffee house, old gentleman in coffee room. Waiter says I, I wish to smoke a cigar, have you a smoking room. *W.* No occasion sir, you can smoke here. *I.* (*to* O.G.) Perhaps it may be disagreeable to you sir, in which case— *O.G.* By no means. I'm myself a smoker (laying aside specs, and looking like Cosmogony: Jenkins-) *I.* I have good Cigars, will you d. m. t. f. to accept of one. *O.G.* Very kind. *I.* Come from Calais? *O.G.* Boulogne. Go to Bristol. *I.* Anche io sono Bristoliano. *O.G.* Know King? *I.* Wife my aunt. *O.G.* Are you? *I.* Son of well-known physician at Clifton. *O.G.* Not of Dr B.? *I.* Same unworthily. *O.G.* That's curious. Your brother married my niece a fortnight ago. *I.* Happy man! Hear of it now for ye first time. Tories will never be my heirs. *O.G.* O! G—! (reassumes specs and exit.) *I.* I! *exeo.*

Good joke at Canterbury. I visit an old schoolfellow, who has become high church, tory, and not being quite up to German, an admirer of F. Schlegel. I said that this fellow was become many years before his Ω plaudite, a political renegade, a catholic pro formâ, a mystical writer, and a mercenary scribe for the holy alliance. As we parted he wished me good night and requested me never to visit him again, if I should chance to pass through Canterbury. You may judge therefore how likely the gentlemen of Charterhouse are to patronize my rhymed enormities in the same measure, in w^h the Etonians have supported the innocent verses of your loving cousin. And here closeth this epistle. I shall hardly write again before I have finished my book: w^h grows as slowly as a yew tree at present: the chapters on hand requiring a light hearted sunniness of style, w^h I can only command when the birds are singing, and sun is shining on morning dew. Yours

T. L. B.

116

I hope to hear from you again before I return to England & w^d request you to send me a copy of a song w^h you recom[m]end: I wish to be prodigal of lyrics & have only about 22-23 as yet: one or two of w^h are of doubtful merit. In this confounded weather the coldblooded frogs themselves hardly have the heart to sing out their love thoughts.

What do you say to the new dramatists. An article in the Dublin review, w^h I looked thro' a day or two ago, contains extracts w^h certainly indicate a beating of the pulse, a warming of the skin, and a sigh or two from the dramatic lady muse, as if she were about to awake from her asphyxy of a hundred years. And ye Examiner is quite rapturous about Strafford: altho' I confess that the extracts, he chooses and praises appear to me not exactly dramatic. One is a dialogue between two people describing Pym's appearance, action &c in a style w^h has been approved of by critics of late and considered highly graphic. But it is not very artificial?

In Shak. such passages are rare and only in scenes, where the person whose actions are described must necessarily be laconic if not entirely speechless; and where the spectators in their doubt, fear, & wonder naturally communicate to each other their interpretations of the dumb show before them. For instance in Hamlet where the ghost, unwilling or unable perhaps to speak to his son in the presence of Horatio & the watch motions him to follow. It is of some consequence to settle one's opinion on a question of this nature. I am not sure that I am right, but I doubt: What say you? And now I leave you to your parchment joys

T. L. B.

Addressed to
    T. F. Kelsall Esqre
    Fareham
    Hants

LETTER XLII (Fragment)

To Revell Phillips
Zurich April 28 1938

Dear Phillips,—I have been some weeks employed in translating Mr. Grainger's(74) book on the Spinal Cord into German: the book will be printed probably in the summer: but before that happens I should wish to communicate either personally or by letter with the author on some points, not essentially connected with the enquiry, which have been set in a clearer light by more recent writers. I allude especially to some observations on the microscopic anatomy of the central organs of the nervous system contained in the latter paragraphs of the 2nd chapter, which must be either omitted or altered, inasmuch as it is no longer admitted by the more experienced in these delicate researches that the peculiar form ascribed by Ehenburg, Purkinge &c to the primary medullory fibrils in the brain and in its' dependancy, is to be found in the fresh and uninjured organ.

LETTER XLIII (Fragment)

Zurich May 5ᵗʰ 1839

I am in hopes that I shall at length conclude an arrangement with a very eminent publisher concerning the appearance of the translation of Mr. Grainger's work, of which I know not whether I should say I am glad or sorry that no German version has as yet appeared.

LETTER XLIV (Fragment)

To Revell Phillips
Zurich Septʳ 12, 1839

Dear Phillips,—You will probably already have read of the catastrophe of Zurich last Friday (the 8ᵗʰ) about 6000 of the peasantry of this canton, half unarmed, and the other half armed with scythes, dungforks & poles, led on by a mad fanatic, and aided by some traitors in the cabinet, and many in the town, effected the downfall of the government, by far the best and most liberal that the canton ever lived under.

One of the most distinguished men, both in science and politics, Hegetschweiler,(75) himself one of the most important members of the government, was shot in the tumult, and buried to day. Kellar was compelled to flee and is at present in a neighbouring republic; where I visited him; he desired to be remembered to you. Besides him many of the most eminent of the republic have been obliged to seek safety elsewhere.

These disorders bordering on absolute anarchy will

119

account for my not having been able to execute the deeds and dispatch them before to-morrow as the communications were not safe. In consequence of this state of things, in which neither property nor person is secure I shall find it necessary to give up my present residence entirely. Indeed the dispersion of my friends and acquaintance all of whom belonged to the liberal party renders it nearly impossible for me to remain longer here.

LETTER XLV

To Thomas Forbes Kelsall
Giessen Novr 13 1844

My dear Kelsall,—I deferred answering your letter, which I duly received in Baden n^r Zurich, in August, till I sh^d be able to say where I should fix for some time. Altho' my arrangements are not yet completed it is likely that I shall remain here at least the winter. Of course you know that Liebig's chemical school is in this wretched little town: and wishing to avail myself of his instructions I have come to it.

My journey brought me thro' Basel, where Paracelsus (not Mr. Browning's) (the historical P. was a complete charlatan, seldom sober, clever and cunning, living on the appetite of his contemporaneous public for the philosopher's stone and the universal medicine; castrated as a child by the jaws of a pig, all his life a vagabond, who at last died drunk in his single shirt at Salzburg:) where P. burnt Galen's works openly as professor of the university, beginning the medical reform so, as Luther did that in religion by his public conflagration of the bull launched against him.

P. was a poetical fellow in his way certainly, and in his writings a wholesale dealer in a certain style, of which every prudent verse-manufacturer will avail himself sparingly; no

120

doubt the epithet given to that sort of flowers of eloquence was derived from one of his names, for he had many, as he might often need an alias, and when he wrote at full, denominated himself Philippus Aureolus Theophrastus paracelsus Bombastus ab Hohenheim. He was born at Hohenheim near Einsiedeln in the canton Schwyz and his surname was probably Bombast. But the memory of P. has passed away with the dance of Death, and the old university, whose walls echoed once to the voices of Vesalius, Oecolampadius, Melanchthon and Erasmus, is just pulled down to make way for a new building in which teachers of mediocrity will soon dictate to empty benches.

Basel has retained a good collection of Holbeins, who was a native of the town where they tell odd stories of him. He was employed once in painting a ceiling for a patrician, who was somewhat stingy, and knowing how apt the master was to slip from his aerial perch into a vintner's to enjoy himself, he left his counting-house every vacant minute to assure himself that the painter's legs were dangling in their proper place from the scaffold. H. could not endure such constraint, and to be able to absent himself unperceived painted a pair of very sober legs against the wall, which he left as his proxy while his own were enjoying themselves under the tippling bench. This monument of his ingenuity remained till within a few years but every leg has it's end and we have nothing left but a leg-end of those of Holbein.

I will spare you all remarks on the liver-pasties and fortifications of Strasburg, the monotony of Manheim, and the militaries of Mainz: referring you to Murray etc. In Frankfort the new monument of Goethe was just unveiled: it is a Bronze designed by Schwanthaler, and admirably executed: the pedestal ornamented in haut relief with groups out of his principal fictions: as Mignonne, W. Meister, and the harper:—Hermann and Dorothea, (stiff and disagreeable, perhaps purposely modelled so by the artist, as characteristic of that soporific composition:) Faust and Meph, Iphigenia, Orestes and Thoas, Egmont, Gotz, Erlking, Bride of Corinth, etc, all graceful and harmonious. G. turns his back to the Francfort Theatre, why, I do not know: he certainly w^d if he

121

was alive, for the actors are almost as bad as the English: always with the exception of Dem. Lindner and my old friend Weidner, with whom I helped to keep his 66th birthday, celebrating the same with a German sonnet, w[h] no doubt you are not in the least anxious to see, so I'll sing you another song, w[h] I believe is new to you—I have stuck it into the endless J. B.

1.

In lover's ear a wild voice cried:
   "Sleeper, awake and rise!"
A pale form stood by his bedside,
   With heavy tears in her sad eyes.
A beckoning hand, a moaning sound,
A new-dug grave in weedy ground
For her who sleeps in dreams of thee.
Awake. Let not the murder be.
Unheard the faithful dream did pray,
And sadly sighed itself away.
Sleep on,—sung Sleep—, to-morrow,
Tis time to know thy sorrow.
Sleep on, sung Death, to-morrow
From me thy sleep thou'lt borrow
Sleep on, lover, sleep on
   The tedious dream is gone
     The bell tolls one.

2.

Another hour, another dream,
Awake, awake, it wailed
Arise, ere with the moon's last beam
Her dearest life hath paled
A hidden light, a muffled tread,
A daggered hand beside the bed
Of her who sleeps in dreams of thee

122

Thou wak'st not: let the murder be.
    In vain the faithful &c
    Sleep on, love, sleep on
    The tedious dream is gone
        Soon comes the sun.

3

Another hour, another dream.
A red wound on a snowy breast,
A rude hand stifling the last scream
On rosy lips a death-kiss pressed.
Blood on the sheets, blood on the floor,
The murderer stealing thro' the door.
Now said the voice with comfort deep
She sleeps indeed & thou mayst sleep
The scornful dream: then turned away
To the first bleeding cloud of day
Sleep on; sung Sleep &c
Sleep on lover, sleep on,
    The tedious dream is gone,
        The murder's done.

Also; to fill up:—

1.

The swallow leaves her nest,
The soul my weary breast
But therefore let the rain
        On my grave
Fall pure. For why complain,
Since both will come again
        O'er the wave ?

> The wind dead leaves & snow
> Doth hurry to and fro,
> And once a day shall break
>   O'er the wave
> When a storm of ghosts shall shake
> The dead until they wake
>   In the grave.

Do not imagine that I do much in the pottery way now. Sometimes to amuse myself I write you a German lyric or epigram right scurrilous, many of w^h have appeared in the Swiss and German papers & some day or other I shall have them collected and printed for fun. As for publishing in England I am not inclined that way: the old J. B., repeatedly touched up, is a strange conglomerate, and I have not since had time or inclination to begin a right tragedy. Altogether the old thing in its present shape may be hardly worse, than the most that's presented to the public, but that w^d be in my opinion no excuse for printing it.

All the rhymes I have seen many a year are not worth the rags they are printed on: and I think myself entitled to the thanks of the British public for not having bothered them the last 20 years. Recollect, I might have written as much as R. Montgomery: and have forborne. I am happy to hear that you have a decent edition of Shakspeare. From what you say, I must however suspect that Knight has not acted candidly towards the Germans. That is very foolish; for who does not understand German nowadays, who is not acquainted with German literature since Lessing? Always excepting Mr. Carlyle.

The hypothesis as to the authorship of the two noble kinsmen belongs to Tieck originally, and no doubt Knight has availed himself of that Shakspearian Critic's arguments. I have no books at hand, and the work in w^h it at first appeared does not occur to me. But the singular supposition that Chapman sh^d be the third dramatist concerned therein, w^h

always appeared to me highly improbable, has prevented me from forgetting it. Very likely the passage occurs in T.'s criticism on Hamlet. The work appears to me more like Dekkers or even Ben's: Chapman is surely one of the Elizabethans who has the least dramatic talent: but I begin to forget all these things.

T.'s works contain a vast deal of excellent observations on W.S. & have no doubt been well plundered by the author of a biography. T. is here as in every respect far superior to W. A. Schlegel, whose name by the way I do not pronounce Sklegel now: so that you see I have learnt something in Germany.

Frankfurt aƒm
    Hôtel de Landsberg
        4ᵗʰ Jan. 1845

Liebig had no room; so I went to Berlin. There we had a week of royal fun. One day they inaugurated the new opera-house and the next chopped off Tscheck's head—And was not that a dainty dish etc? The Prussians, and particularly F. W. IV, always disgust me very soon, so I called on my way, on Saxony, and then came here to stay 6—8 weeks till March *e.g.*,

I have looked at your letter again and am *not* convinced by that it is my business to get anything printed. 20 years ago I was so overrated, that of course I must fall short of all reasonable and unreasonable expectation. Times are much changed it is true. I am not aware that there's one single fellow who has the least nose for poetry that writes. You seem to take Tealeaves for Bay: which is all very natural and Chinese, according to the national Anthem,

Drink. Britannia, Britannia drink your Tea,
For Britons, bores and buttered Toast! they all begins
      with B.

Verily, verily I say unto you amid the lyrical chirpings of your young English sparrows, shall come an eagle, and fetch fire from the altar Miltonic to relight the dark-Lanterns of Diogenes and Guy Fawkes. As to the who, where and when of the prophecy, axe Moore of the almanac. Few are called this day, and none are chosen. Doth the Imaum sing out Past tin acock & a rainy night (Charley Knight?), and saith the watchman Allah il Allah? Is the voice that crieth in the Wilderness a penny crumpet?

The solution some day next century.

Yours T. L. B.

As to real Poetry

I have oft thought,
Thou art so beautiful above all women,
I might be you; but yet 'tis happier still
To be another, to admire and love thee

as the author of D^s J. B says
somewhere or other.

Addressed to
T. F. Kelsall Esqre
Solicitor
Fareham
Hants
England

To Thomas Forbes Kelsall
Shiffnall Aug 11. 1846.

My dear Kelsall,—I have been in the native land of the unicorn, about a week and may remain 5 more: I should wish to see and talk with you during my stay. As you are the busy man I leave the arrangements to your convenience. I had no time to visit Procter in passing through London, but am told that he is appointed to a high(76) office in the government of the kingdom of ye moon, upon which, as a retired member of the company of poets he was I suppose accustomed to draw liberally.

I saw R. Phillips, of course, who w^d desire to be remembered to you, were he here: he is stout morally and physically in spite of the undeserved blows, which blind Fate has showered on him. Poor J. G. H. Bourne, another honest and industrious man, has broken down under the pressure of grievances and has left a large young family behind him. These are all our common acquaintance I believe. As for myself, the world which I have carefully kept at arms length has only made me somewhat more indifferent and prosaic than before. Direct to me Francis Beddoes Esqre Cheney Longville n^r Ludlow, and find out someway of convincing yourself of the identity, of w^h I am not quite sure, of your old and present friend

T. L. Beddoes

Addressed to
    Thomas Kelsall Esqre
        Fareham
            Hants

To Thomas Forbes Kelsall
Catherine S^t
Grange Road
Birkenhead
[Postmark] Mr 10 1847

My dear Kelsall,—I have been detained since you had the kindness to answer a letter of mine (Aug 13.) much to my distaste in this extraordinary part of the world: and am now staying in one of the most abominable places this side of Tartarus, till it shall please the apple blossom to appear. I meditate still an incursion on your privacy before I leave the Britannic shores, of which I will apprize you some days in advance.

It will give me very great pleasure to confer with you, but pray expect no addition to your experience from the scenes of my existence; nothing can be more monotonous, dull and obscure: the needy knife grinder's adventures would have been oriental marvels and pantomimic mysteries in comparison. Prose of the leadenest drab dye has ever pursued your humble servant. But of that you will not doubt, —I believe I might have met with some success as a retailer of small coal, or a writer of long-bottomed tracts, but doubt of my aptitude for any higher literary or commercial occupation. But you will see—I believe I have all the dulness, if not the other qualities—of your British respectability.

You have been always good enough to overrate any bit of verse &c I scribbled, so that I was almost tempted to send you something to go thro' at leisure,—or treat like any other drug, I might be unfortunate enough to prescribe—per post, as postage is cheap; but I find that I have lost or left behind nearly all the very little that I have committed to paper in English since last I communicated with you: and what I have is either utterly illegible, or mere refacciamenti of the unhappy Jest book, so that I am compelled to spare you.

I hope to see you well, and as happy as a man ought to be; and to make pleasant new acquaintance among the to me unknown new generation of Kelsalls: and may they flutter and sing in those sunny places of the green wood of life from which our shadows have passed away. Pray say whether it will be still convenient to you to see, in 3 weeks or a month for a hour or a day,

Yours truly
T. L. Beddoes

Addressed to
  T. F. Kelsall Esq[re]
  Fareham
  Hants

LETTER XLVIII

To Thomas Forbes Kelsall
Harcourt Bdgs.,
Temple,
London,
May 29, 1847

My dear Kelsall,—The author of all those celebrated unwritten productions, amongst which I particularly solicit your attention to a volume of letters to yourself, will leave the station for Fareham at seven o'clock to-morrow, and stay Sunday at that place:

Poor bird, that cannot ever
Dwell high in tower of song:
Whose heart-breaking endeavour
But palls the lazy throng.
                                    T. L. B.

LETTER XLIX

To a Relative
Basel Oct 9 1848

My dear A——,—I should have written to you sometime ago, if I had not unfortunately rather unpleasant news regarding myself to report. Do not, I beg of you, regard the matter on its melancholy side alone, for myself I am quite reconciled to my situation and only dread comforters and condolers.

Late in the summer, in July, I fell with a horse in a precipitious part of the neighbouring hills and broke my left leg all to pieces. In spite of the very best treatment part of the fractured limb was obliged to be sacrificed: (I beg your pardon for this style, but I am writing on my back;) and a month ago the lower part of the leg (below the knee joint) was taken off. Thanks to the power of beneficial Chloroform I felt not the least twitch of pain during the operation, and since then I have been slowly but with sure steps advancing in the way of recovery; and before long hope to dot and go one. As soon as I am quite well I shall return to England, but I fear the winter may intervene.

You ask me to recommend you a German book, but do not say on what kind of subject or in what department of literature: & even if you had, I sh^d find it hazardous, because tastes & habits, or trains of thought and study render such different things interesting to different individuals. Dreary & dull is dear Mr. Schopenhauer, and Henrik Steffens tells as little truth as possible, I wot in his *erlebtend*. He has writ some tolerable novels though, sketches of Hyperborean Norwegian life, "Die 4 Norweger" and "Malcolm and Walseth," (or "Walseth and Leith," I forget which,) but if you wish to read goodish Memoirs, very well written, ask for Varnhagen von Ense. Have you not read his book about his wife, the wonderful Berlin Jewess, Rahel, (that is the title of his work,)?

This Rahel Robert was really a woman of great talent, and never printed anything during his [*sic*] life, without the affectation and mendacious vanity of the ginger bread Bettine Brentano. I think Sternberg is one of the best novelists, (a Tieckianer) and then you can read the rather lengthy but well laboured novels (in 3 vols accord⁸ to the English Canon) of the late Frau von Paalzaw—Thomas Thyrnan, St. Roche, Godwic Castle & others. Besides there is Auerbach with *Schwarzwalder Dorpgeschichten, very* good, but some black-forest dialect, tho' not enough to bore you much.

Did you ever enquire for the *reisenden Maler* by Ernest Wagner, a contemporary of old Wolfgang Goethe? It is one of the best German novels. I do not know why people are always a reading new books. Like new bread 'tis not always the most digestible stuff they are baked of; especially, as you say, in French literature, but the French have nothing since the settling of their language in its present form, (for of course I do not deny the genius of Cl. Marot, Jodelle, Rabelais, Montaigne &c) but Moliere, Le Sage, Beaumarchais &c and the Memoirs, Sevignè included, which are interesting and delightful reading.

I am just employed on St. Simons Memˢ of Louis XIV and the Regent, and learn ten-times more about the former than from Voltaire. As to Harbers Innocent III, pray recollect that I think of it as a most learned work as opposed to the light manufactures of Ranke on similar subjects. You must not forget either that H. became privately Catholic while he was Antistes (so the Zwinglians call their Bishops) of

Schaffhausen, a protestant see; I believe that his con- or per-version was occasioned by his researches for his work on that great Pope, and you allmost trace his growing inclination for Rome thro' the volumes. They are rather *hard* reading, being packed so closely with facts, and the style is overladen & J. Müllerish. Read also Gervinus 'Geschichte d. National-literatur der Deutschen.'

Good bye
T. L. B.

LETTER L

To a Relative
Direct under cover to
Monsr A. Frey Med D[r]
à l'Hopital, Basle
Basle
Wednesday Novr 8 1848

My dear A—— ,—Do not think me incapable of appreciating your offer of visiting me here, if I resolve not to avail myself of it. In the first place I object to the journey, which is free neither from difficulty nor danger in the present state of Germany, at this time of year &c 2[ndly] You must remember that I am in a hospital, (a very pleasant one, with a large garden into which my window looks,) that strange visitors are only admitted during the day, and you know how short that is; besides I do not wish to remain here a very long time: & when you arrived I might very likely be preparing to leave. I therefore beg you to allow me to decline your proposal without suspecting me of being ungrateful. I am going on well, sit up during the day, and am just beginning to learn to walk.

One feels rather uncertain about Ranke's merit or

132

demerits as a writer, because perhaps what appears worthy either of praise or censure may not be properly attributable to him. One of his earliest works was a critical survey of the Italian Epic poets, in which an English reviewer (Ed. or Quarterly?) detected an extensive series of acknowledged quotations from Panizzi's introductory volume to his London Edition of the till then rare Orlando of Bojardo. I do not know whether the criticism was taken notice of in Germany, but it appeared rather a shabby affair; and I have felt a disinclin^n to read anything of that writer since.

Lately there have been some audacious instances of plagiarism among the younger German authors, wh. have been sufficiently blamed. The learned were sufficiently abusive of Wagenfeld when he published his false Janchoniathon, because that in genious literary forgery had been considered genuine by some of their most celebrated philologians. But surely a literary theft is at least equally reprehensible.

Who are now living at Edgeworth's town? St. Paul's ranks higher than Christ's Hospital, I believe, and Emmeline is therefore fortunate in obtaining a presentation for her boy, if she is at as little expense as at the latter school. A clever, diligent youth has a fair chance of a scholarship, I believe, at Oxford.

A new collection of letters from Goëthe to a Frau v. Stein has just issued; they were written during the last century & appear to be interesting. The great superiority of the Germans in their poetical literature consists however in their translations. Voss's Homer, particularly the Odyssee, (read if possible the first edition of that, or a reprint of the same, because he injured it afterwards by improvements & corrections) Griess' Ariosto, Tasso & Calderon, Regiss' Bojardo, Rabelais, Cid, Droyssen's Æschylus &c are vastly preferable to any translation I know in English, excepting perhaps Motteux' (who by the way was French by birth & education) continuation & revisal of Sir I. Urquharts Rabelais.

An acquaintance of mine has taken the trouble to translate Uhland's Poems,(77) but in want of a London

133

publisher was obliged to print at Frankfort $^{o}/_{m}$; with the exception of a very few gross blunders his version is correct as well as his versification; and he was wise enough to keep to the metres of his original, even where the hexameter was before him: but he has too much of the conventional poetical language of the fashionable modern potters to please me. It was a difficult and no doubt tedious task, for Uhland's poetry is nothing but language well coloured, phraseology drearily deserted by ideas.

> Yours truly
> T. L. B.
> *Novr 10*

I am getting on very well.

Addressed to
Miss ——
    West Town
      Bristol

To Revell Phillips
[*January 26 1849*]

My dear Phillips,—I am food for what I am good for—worms. I have made a will here which I desire to be respected, and add the donation of £20 to Dr Ecklin my physician.

W. Beddoes must have a case (50 bottles) of Champagne Moet 1847 growth to drink my death in.

Thanks for all kindness. Borrow the £200. You are a good & noble man & your children must look sharp to be like you.

Yours,
if my own,
ever,
T. L. B.

Love to Anna, Henry, the Beddoes of Longvill and Zoe and Emmeline King—also to Kelsall whom I beg to look at my MSS. and print or not as he thinks fit. I ought to have been among other things a good poet. Life was too great a bore on one peg and that a bad one. Buy for Dr Ecklin above mentioned [*one of*] Reade's best stomach-pumps.

[*This note, written in pencil, was found folded on the poet's bosom, as he lay insensible after taking poison, in his bed in the Town Hospital of Basel. He died at 10 p.m. the same night.*]

NOTES

1. John Hunt, the journalist and publisher, brother of Leigh Hunt. He had recently brought the Liberal to a close.

2. The "Shelley affair" was the publication of Shelley's *Posthumous Poems* in 1824, the part taken in which by Beddoes is several times referred to in the course of these letters.

3. Bryan Waller Procter, "Barry Cornwall," though much Beddoes' senior, being at this time in his thirty-seventh year, was the most intimate of all the literary associates of the latter, and remained to the last his faithful friend. He had in 1824 already published almost all the works by which he is generally known.

4. No doubt the 1820 edition of Prometheus Unbound.

5. C. E. Walker wrote several very successful pseudo-poetical tragedies, such as *Wallace, The Briton Chief*, and, in particular, *The Warlock of the Glen*, of which Thackeray gives so funny an analysis.

6. *Britain's Ida*, a poem published under the name of Spenser in 1628, now commonly attributed to the youth of Phineas Fletcher.

7. *The Last Man*, a tragedy projected by Beddoes, but never finished.

8. "Bernard the Quaker"; Bernard Barton, a member of the Society of Friends and a minor poet. He was one of Beddoes' pet aversions.

9. George Darley (1795-1846), the dramatic critic of the *London Magazine* under the signature of John Lacy; and afterwards more distinguished as the author of *Sylvia*, the *May Queen*, and other dramatic poems.

10. Eventually no portrait was used. I am informed by Lady Shelley that the reason was that Jane Williams, to whom Mary Shelley had lent the sketch which it was proposed to engrave, mislaid it until it was too late.

11. Thomas Jefferson Hogg (1792-1862), the biographer of Shelley.

12. William Godwin.

13. Beddoes was behindhand in his information, since Thomas Love Peacock had married Jane Gryffydh, the "Welsh turtle," in March 1820.

14. John Hamilton Reynolds, the friend of Keats and Hood.

15. This refers to the Notes from the *Pocket-Book of a late Opium-Eater*, which De Quincey was at this time beginning to contribute to Taylor and Hessey's *London Magazine*.

16. The *Second Maiden's Tragedy*, which was then just for the first time printed from a manuscript in the Lansdowne Collection, was, and remains, a great mystery. It was licensed in October, 161 1. On the back of the MS. a contemporary hand had written "William Goughe"; the first of these names had been erased, and "Thomas" substituted. "Thomas Goughe" had then been struck through, and "George Chapman" written. Finally "Will. Shakespear," had been substituted. Modern criticism has conjectured that either Chapman or Cyril Tourneur was the author. It is interesting to see that Beddoes instantly perceived the great poetical value of this obscure drama.

17. Sir Timothy Shelley, the poet's father.

18. Charles Robert Mathurin (1782-1824), the author of *Melmoth the Wanderer*, He died three weeks after the date of this letter.

19. George Croly was at this time writing much for the Literary Gazette, and had lately brought out a new play, Cataline, but it was a tragedy, not a comedy.

20. *Hans Beet-pot's Invisible Comedy of See Me and See Me Not* was published in quarto, 1618, by Danbridgecourt Belchier.

21. Thomas Campbell had just published his *Theodric*, a performance which had proved a sad disappointment to his admirers.

22. William Lisle Bowles, the sonneteer and forerunner of the romantic movement.

23. *The Fatal Dowry*, a tragedy begun by Field, completed by Massinger, and published in 1632.

24. The beginning, it would seem, of what ultimately became *Death's Jest-Book*.

25. This volume was anonymous, and Coleridge thought that Lamb had written it. The authorship of Hood and Reynolds was soon revealed.

26. It is strange that the youthful Praed should already be known by name to Beddoes, who probably refers to his contributions to *The Etonian*.

27. The Rev. John Moultrie, born in 1804.

28. Sir Francis Chantrey, R.A., the sculptor.

29. Johann Friedrich Blumenbach, the first great German zoologist. Born in 1752, he had been since 1778 professor at Göttingen, where he was to die in 1840.

30. Lord Byron.

31. "Pygmalion, or the Cyprian Statuary," was one of Beddoes' most ambitious exercises in narrative blank verse. The "Oxford magaziners" seem to have rejected it, and it made its first appearance in the *Poems* of 1851.

32. Moultrie.

33. Friedrich Stromeyer, born in 1776. He was a very eminent chemist, had been professor of chemistry at Göttingen since 1810, and was to die in 1835.

34. The remainder of the 1820 edition of Shelley's Prometheus Unbound was still on sale, and was to remain so for many years.

35. The *Bride's* (or *Brides'*) *Tragedy*, published by Beddoes when he was still at Oxford, in 1822.

36. Georg Friedrich Benecke (1762-1844), librarian at Göttingen, and a copious writer on early German literature, on which he was a leading authority.

37. "Barry Cornwall,"—B. W. Procter.

38. This was the sensational landscape by John Martin, afterwards exhibited in the West Room of the Royal Academy (No. 403) in 1837.

39. A reference to Darley's dramatic miscellany, called The *Labours of Idleness*, 1826.

40. The very mild lucubrations of the Quaker poet had just been rewarded by an annuity from his co-religionists.

41. William Jerdan, the active and influential editor of the

Literary Gazette.

42. Konrad Johann Martinus Langenbeck, born in 1778, was a celebrated anatomist and surgeon. He had been professor of anatomy at Göttingen since 1814.

43. Arnold Hermann Ludwig Heeren, the leading German historian of his day, was born in 1760. In 1824-26 he was publishing his greatest work, the *Ideen über Politik*. He died in 1842.

44. Gustav Hugo, the eminent jurist and professor of Roman law (1764-1844). Hugo had held the chair of jurisprudence at Gottingen since 1792.

45. Friedrich Bouterwek (1766-1828). Since 1802 professor of philosophy at Göttingen. His interesting autobiography had appeared in 1818.

46. *The Improvisatore*, a collection of lyrical poems, printed in 1821, was Beddoes' first publication.

47. John Eagles, of Bristol, author of *The Sketcher*, published in *Blackwood* from 1833 to 1835. He had previously been Sydney Smith's curate.

48. On the 12th of October, Leigh Hunt and his family had returned from their too-famous visit to Italy.

49. Just a year before this was written, Charles Lamb had "come home *forever*" and was now quietly rusticating at Enfield.

50. Johann Tobias Mayer (1752-1830), son of the famous astronomer of the same name, had been professor of mathematics at Göttingen since 1790.

51. Ernst Benjamin Salamon Raupach was the most prolific German dramatist of his age. He was born in 1784. At the time Beddoes wrote, Dr. Raupach had enjoyed a great success with his *Die Freunde*, 1825, and *Isidor von Olga*, 1826.

52. Jean Paul Richter died on the 14th of November, 1825.

53. This may refer to Lord Gifford, at that time dying. He would doubtless be known to Beddoes, at Bristol, of which city he had been Recorder, as Sir Robert Gifford.

54. In Ben Jonson's comedy of *Epicene*.

55. Robert Pearse Gillies, the friend of Sir Walter Scott, and the Kemperhausen of the *Noctes*, supplied abundant translations of German literature to *Blackwood's.*

56. "Heber" must be a jocose mode of spelling "Hebrew."

57. "Avarice, Sir Walter." This is a striking proof of the degree to which Scott's noble efforts to recover his financial position were misunderstood. At the very moment when Beddoes was penning this unfortunate phrase, the Chronicler of the Canongate was struggling against the designs of the Israelites, and preparing for "Calton Jail or a trip to the Isle of Man."

58. John G. H. Bourne, an early friend of Beddoes and Procter. He published a poem called *England Won* in 1845. Beddoes mentions his death as occurring in 1846.

59. Robert Montgomery, who had published his *Omnipresence of the Deity* in 1828.

60. Allan Cunningham began in 1829 to issue an annual, called *The Anniversary*, to which various people of distinction contributed.

61. Willem Bilderdijk, the Dutch poet, born in 1756, died in 1831.

62. *The Briton Chief* was a very popular tragedy by C. E. Walker, produced in 1823.

63. Ludwig Holberg, called the Father of Danish literature, was born at Bergen in Norway in 1684. He died at Sorö in Denmark, in 1754. His works are encyclopaedic in range, but it is by his brilliant comedies that he is now best remembered.

64. Bernhard Severin Ingemann, the Danish poet, born in 1789, and died in 1862.

65. Leopold Schafer, the lyrical poet and novelist, was born in 1784.

66. These were the "Lines written in a copy of *Prometheus Unbound*" which had appeared in the *Athenæum* for May 18.

67. Johann Lukas Schoenlein, born in 1793, was one of the first clinical authorities of Germany. He had been professor at Würzburg since 1824.

68. This volume was to have been entitled *The Ivory Gate*, but it was never sent to press.

69. George Darley, now utterly out of sympathy with his own earlier predilections, was writing truculent reviews in the

140

Athenæum.

70. Bourne.

71. Haynes Bayly's *Weeds of Witchery*, a feeble collection of songs, had just appeared.

72. Walter Savage Landor's *Citation and Examination of William Shakespear*, published anonymously in 1834.

73. *Cosmo dei Medici* was a blank verse tragedy by Richard Hengist Home.

74. Richard Dugard Grainger, a young surgeon of great promise, had published in 1837, a very original volume *On the Spinal Cord*. Nothing is now known of Beddoes' German translation.

75. Hegetschweiler. This name has by Beddoes' previous editors (myself included) been mis-spelt Hegetochweiber, the reference being thus concealed to Johann Hegetschweiler, the distinguished Swiss patriot and botanist. He was born in 1789, gave up his scientific pursuits for the sake of politics in 1830, and on the 8th of September 1839 was shot in the streets of Zurich by one of the peasants who were invading the town.

76. Procter had long been an annually nominated Metropolitan Commissioner of Lunacy, but under the new Act he was now appointed one of the permanent commission. He resigned this post in 1861.

77. This was the version of Uhland's poems, with a biography and notes, published by A. Platt in 1848.